Redirecting Children's Behavior

KATHRYN J. KVOLS

THIRD EDITION | REVISED

PARENTING PRESS, INC.
Seattle, Washington

First edition, 1979
Second edition, 1993
Third edition, 1998

Edited by Carolyn J. Threadgill
Cover and text design by Magrit Baurecht Design
Printed in the United States of America

10 9

Library of Congress Cataloguing-in-Publication Data
Kvols, Kathryn J., 1952–
    Redirecting children's behavior / by Kathryn J. Kvols.
– – 3rd ed., rev.
      p. cm.
    Rev. ed. of: Redirecting children's misbehavior / Bill &
Kathy Kvols-Riedler. c1979.
    Includes bibliographical references and index.
    ISBN 1-884734-31-6 (library)
    ISBN 1-884734-30-8 (pbk.)
    1. Child rearing. 2. Child psychology. I. Riedler, Bill.
Redirecting children's misbehavior. II. Title.
HQ772.K83 1998   97-37464
649's . 1--DC21   CIP

Parenting Press, Inc.
P.O. Box 75267
Seattle, Washington 98125

"Lord, make

me an instrument

of thy peace."

–St. Francis of Assisi

Acknowledgments

First and foremost, I would like to thank my family: my husband, Brian, for endless support, love, and gentle nudging; my son Tyler, who taught me what unconditional love means; Brianna, who helps me remember to be silly; Chloee, Amy, Emily, and Cindy Harper, who are teaching me what it means to be a blended family.

Thank you, also, to my former husband Bill Riedler, who co-authored the first edition of this book. I especially appreciate the great father he is to our son Tyler.

A very special thank you goes to all the instructors of the "Redirecting Children's Behavior" course, who have encouraged and supported me for many years. Bob Hoekstra, Tim and Ann Jordan, Helen Hall, Lucinda Hudgins, Lisa Lakner, and Carol Watson are but a few who inspired me in this work. Betty Towry has been a great friend, as well as my confidante.

I acknowledge the late Rudolf Dreikurs, M.D. for being the source of inspiration for *Redirecting Children's Behavior.*

Contents

Foreword

What we know and believe about children and families has changed dramatically in the last twent-five years. Parents, teachers, and coaches recall the "good old days" when you could tell kids to do something, and they jumped and did it! Kids today, on the other hand, are requesting respect and democracy, especially in the autocracies which control their homes, classrooms, and athletic fields. The result is confusion and power struggles with parents and professionals and, often, we don't know why we're struggling.

If you step back and look at the progress we've made in understanding children, it's astonishing how far we've come in the last quarter of a century. It was not until the late 1960's and early 1970's, through the work of Dr. T. Barry Brazelton and others, that we became aware that infants could see, hear, feel, and actively contribute to their relationships with their parents. How magnificent! With this finding, we began to view children, even at the beginning of their lives, as participants in the family process. Children have become powerful, emphatic collaborators to be respected versus clay for us to mold and control. It's no wonder that many of us have experienced confusion and chaos.

So here is Kathryn Kvols's book, *Redirecting Children's Behavior,* offering us the tools we need to develop the closeness with our children and families that we want so very much. Kathryn believes, as I do, that every person is born whole, perfect, and connected to everyone and everything. Through experiences as children, with parents, siblings, and others, we are socialized and wounded in ways that cause us to lose our awareness of the connections with others. This book offers us the means to reconnect. It provides the framework and process for parenting so that we learn to relate with children in a way that supports their development, creating adults who feel whole and free and able to experience closeness and intimacy with others.

–Timothy J. Jordan, M.D.

Why I Wrote This Book

Children have the ability to touch the very depths of our souls. One moment we're feeling love and joy; the next moment, frustration and incompetence and, at times, despair. The purpose of this book is twofold: to help you create a warmer, closer relationship with your child that increases love and joy and to teach you new skills that help you when you feel like you can't cope.

People are becoming aware that fear or force are ineffective tools to motivate others, both in business and in our families. We often feel frustrated when we don't know what else to do as our children push us against the wall. When we're running late and our two-year-old refuses to get in her car seat or our teenagers openly defy us, we wonder how to respond so as to do no harm, act according to our values, and teach kids what they need to learn.

When we reach into our bag of tricks, we often come up with methods that our parents used when raising us, or we settle on an expedient solution. These responses often don't produce the results we want.

The suggestions in this book are based on more than twenty years of personal experience teaching courses on parenting, lecturing, counseling, and teaching kids in summer camps and school. I have heard thousands of parents, teachers, and counselors voice their concerns and frustrations over the children in their care. It is my goal, through this book and the parent education I do, to help parents raise self-motivated and responsible children, who are able to win another's cooperation, create and maintain close relationships, and work successfully on teams.

Redirecting children's behavior is a form of discipline that helps parents raise children in a peaceful and respectful way; it is firm and kind. Its goal is for the child to assume responsibility for his or her actions and to become motivated from within rather than by external circumstances or events. The redirecting principle defines discipline as guidance and teaching, with an emphasis on mutual respect. This method teaches natural and logical consequences for a child's misbehavior, instead of the use of punishment. As a result, the child gains self-esteem and cooperation skills.

Redirecting children's behavior is a way of life. It focuses on creating win/win situations in which no one is the loser, not the parent, the child, the teacher, the friend, nor the coach. When children sense that you aren't trying to control them, but are rather trying to make both of you winners, they are more respectful and cooperative.

I firmly believe that the family unit is the fabric of which this country is woven. As we create more peace and harmony within families, our society will become more cooperative and experience less violence and isolation. Together, we can make a difference for all children and for our world.

–Kathryn J. Kvols

1

Take Care of Yourself

Your son has just spilled his juice on the carpet. It's no big deal, but you really lose your temper this time. Why do you react so strongly now and not the last time he spilled juice?

One reason we parents become irritable, overwhelmed, depressed, or sick is that we have not been doing a very good job of taking care of ourselves. How long has it been since you had thirty minutes by yourself to do whatever you wanted? Common answers I hear are, "I can't remember," or, "I don't have time to do that."

Just before the airplane takes off, the stewardess instructs parents to place the oxygen mask on themselves first in an emergency and then place a mask on their child. Notice the request: Put yours on first, then you will be able to help your child. All too often we satisfy the needs of our children and others before our own. As a result, our energy is depleted and we have nothing left to give, or we give with resentment and frustration. Even a minor problem challenges our depleted reserves.

Why don't parents take care of themselves? Some important reasons are:

- We've been taught from an early age that it's selfish to take care of ourselves.

- We feel that taking quiet time or "down time" is not good use of our time.

- We don't believe that we deserve time for ourselves alone.

- We believe that we just don't have, or can't find, the time.

- We don't know how to take care of ourselves.

There is much to gain when we take good care of ourselves. We are:

- Refreshed and have more energy for our children.

- More confident and creative when our children spring surprises on us.

- Ready and eager to spend time with our families.

- Teaching our children, by example, how to take care of themselves.

- Sending the message to them that it is not only okay but important that they take care of themselves, now and when they too are parents.

What makes taking care of yourself a challenge?

Parents may be under a number of strains that make self-care a challenge. Some of these strains are self-imposed and some are reactions to what is going on around them. Look through the challenges I've listed to see which describe your situation. Consider the suggestions for relief.

Burnout

When you have no more energy for the demands life makes on you, you suffer from burnout. Look for these symptoms:

- irritability and crankiness
- feeling rushed and overwhelmed
- accident prone
- tired
- overburdened
- sick often
- depressed
- weepy
- resentful

When you feel these signs, you need to take time out for yourself. We'll talk more about how to do that later.

Negative thoughts

The negative thoughts that cause the most trouble are worry, fear, guilt, resentment, and anger. These emotions sap our energy and keep us from being fully present with our children.

Worry

As parents, we often waste energy worrying about a problem, instead of trusting that life will work out. If you are worried, ask yourself, "What action can I take to solve this problem?" Then take action and let go.

When my son, Tyler, was five years old, we were driving up a winding road through a large piece of property purchased for our business. The property was run down and in need of extensive repair before our opening day. My son looked at me and said, "Mommy, what's that face?" This was the question he always asked when I appeared to be discouraged. "I guess I'm worried," I said. "Worried? About what?" I answered, "I'm worried about money." Tyler replied reprovingly, "Mom, don't you know life works?"

Fear

Fear of mistakes paralyzes us and causes us to mistrust our own capabilities. Rudolf Dreikurs, M.D. wrote wisely in *Children: The Challenge:*

The importance of courage in parents cannot be overemphasized. Whenever you feel dismayed or find yourselves thinking, "My gosh, I did it all wrong," be quick to recognize this symptom of your own discouragement . . . you need the "courage to be imperfect." . . . Watch for the little improvements, and when you find them, relax and have faith in your ability to improve further.

Guilt

Guilt is completely ineffective as a behavior modifier. It takes away your self-confidence and doesn't show you how to avoid repeating the same mistake. Instead of feeling guilty about an action, think about what you will do differently next time.

It was the ninth time Mom had asked Sara to quit running in the living room. She was getting very annoyed because Sara seemed to tune her out. So Mom spanked Sara and sent her to her room.

If it were to happen again, Mom decided she would ask Sara once to stop running in the living room. If she didn't, Mom would pick her up gently and take her to the family room or outside.

Anger

Anger is an honest emotion. Most parents get angry at their children. You want to learn to manage your anger and have it work for you rather than against you. Use these five steps to help you manage your anger positively.

ANGER MANAGEMENT

1. *Watch for the early warning signs of anger.* You may get tense somewhere in your body, such as your jaw or stomach, or your hands may start to perspire. These physical signs tell you that you need to take appropriate action.

2. *Acknowledge that you feel angry.* It doesn't help to stuff or deny your anger. Say to yourself, "I feel angry."

3. *Take a break to cool off.* Count to ten, go to your room, take a walk, or otherwise remove yourself emotionally or physically from the situation.

4. *After you have cooled off, take action.* When you take action, you feel less like a victim and more like a person in control of her life.

5. *Tell the person what you're angry about* (might not be possible in some cases): "I'm angry because the kitchen is a mess."

   Unlikely as it sounds, a simple statement of the problem can help solve it. Start with an "I" statement rather than a "you" statement: attack the problem, not the person. Notice that there is no name-calling, blame, or exaggeration in your simple statement of fact.

Resentment

People feel resentful when they have given up something they want or when they do more than their share of the work, or carry more than a reasonable load of responsibility. Learn to stick up for yourself. Say "No" more often and get the help you need.

The day's stresses

Determine what parts of your day are the most stressful. Take steps to counteract the toll on you. Here are some parent solutions:

A father found it extremely stressful to go directly from work to his home where three children, all under the age of six, greeted him. So he made an agreement with his family that he would go to the gym and work out before he came home. By the time he got home, he was more relaxed and in a better frame of mind to be with his wife and children.

A mother of a three-year-old decided that the morning was her most stressfull time. She had a horrible struggle trying to dress her daughter and was often late to work. She decided to get her daughter dressed for preschool the night before. This solved her problem.

A mother of a five-year-old realized she was most stressed when running errands immediately after picking up her daughter from preschool. The time was pure torture because her daughter would whine and fuss, refuse to get out of the car, and then refuse to get back in the car to go! The mother decided to take her daughter to a park and play with her for fifteen minutes before running her errands. After doing this for a week, she reported that her daughter had become more cooperative once she got her mother's full attention for a brief time.

Indecision

When you are wishy-washy about what you want, your children may take advantage of your indecision. This experience was an eye-opener for me:

I couldn't figure out why Tyler wasn't sleeping through the night. He was certainly old enough. He would wake me up in the middle of the night to nurse. I worked full time and I was exhausted. One night I asked myself,

"What might I be doing to encourage Tyler to get up in the middle of the night?" I realized nursing him at that hour was the only time in the day when I was alone with him without thinking of anything else. Part of me really enjoyed our quiet time and he obviously looked forward to it, too.

I decided to continue for the next thirty days with our midnight rendezvous, and then to train Tyler to sleep through the night. At the same time, I also cleared my schedule over the next month so I had more time with Tyler during the day. After thirty days, Tyler "magically" started sleeping through the night.

Our children read our intentions. So, if you have a problem with your children, get clear about what you want to have happen. Your children will sense your clarity of mind as well as your determination to change the situation.

Lack of confidence

Many parents hold beliefs that interfere with their ability to be effective. Concern that our children always like us makes it difficult to set appropriate limits and be firm. We tend to give in to kids' pressures: "Well, all right, I'll buy you the toy if you stop crying." Self-doubt also gets you into trouble when children challenge or threaten your control.

The desire to be indispensable interferes with our desire to raise self-reliant children. At first, we are truly indispensable. Without us, our child would not survive. However, when our children are older, we often do too much for them, either out of desire to have a role in their lives or to avoid the more difficult challenges that confront us as adults. It is easier for us to succeed in the tasks of tying shoes and getting children started on time in the morning than it is to work on our own dreams.

The belief that you must be in control will cause problems when your children threaten or challenge your need for control (as they inevitably will if this is your belief). Whenever you try to make your child do something, you're very likely to have a power struggle on your hands.

As we turn more responsibilities over to our children, it's easy to feel as if we have been fired, or at least sent away on a long vacation. However, our task as parents is to work ourselves out of that job. We must allow our children to experience the successes and failures that teach them self-confidence and self-reliance as they grow.

Lack of self-reflection

Many parenting problems are caused by personal issues that parents need to take care of, rather than their children's misbehavior. Parents need to practice parenting "from the inside out," so to speak. My children have taught me much about how to play, love unconditionally, handle anger, let go of grudges, and find joy in each day. I must have known these things in my own childhood, but have allowed the pressures of adulthood to bury them.

I use my children as my barometer to measure my inner peace. Usually they misbehave when I'm not at peace. I check in with myself (self-reflection) to see what is amiss. Sometimes I find I've been working too hard, haven't taken time for myself, or haven't spent enough time with my family.

At other times parents may find, upon self-reflection, that their children's behavior is bringing up unresolved issues from their own childhoods. I recall when my son started normal exploration of his sexuality, I was concerned and upset. What I figured out was that his behavior brought back painful memories of my childhood exploration and my own parents' intense shaming of me. Consequently, I overreacted to Tyler's normal, healthy exploration.

Have you noticed how a small child gets angry, lets off steam, and then goes on his way? Some of us learned to stuff our anger inside instead. Unacknowledged anger can lead to depression, illness, and resentment. It can surface later on as retaliation toward others. When we have learned to stuff anger, we often respond inappropriately to events and issues in our adult lives. These situations are especially likely to provoke overreaction: children fighting, anyone being angry or crying, poor grades, unfinished chores, money and eating issues. When you have trouble with any of these situations, look back to your childhood family and think about how your parents dealt with them. What did you learn that may be getting in the way now? What do you want your children to learn from the situation that will be healthier for them?

How to cope with the challenges

It is hard to live a joyful life when your cup is almost empty. Take responsibility for filling up that cup and demand less of others to fill it for you. Taking responsibility for your own happiness will also keep you from self-destructive behavior, such as drug addiction, over-eating, complaining, alcoholism, smoking, insufficient exercise, and illness.

Use calming self-talk

One way to make your life more positive is to get rid of discouraging thoughts. I do this by repeating as many times as necessary the phrase, "I am unlimited in power, peace, and love." In time, I find that I have chased away the negative thoughts and replaced them with this positive one.

Elephants on parade in India would pull down poles and do other mischievous things with their trunks as they marched along. Their trainers discovered that if they gave the elephants short poles to carry, the animals were less disruptive. Like the elephant's pole, the repetitive, encouraging phrase can keep your mind from wandering into mischief.

Let go

Another way to get rid of negative thoughts is to let go. To do this, you give a situation your best effort and then let go of the result. You can't control the result, and the more detached you are from it, the more peaceful you will be. Letting go means you trust your own or your child's innate wisdom, even when there is no visible evidence of it!

Let go when you are angry, worried, feeling guilty or resentful; when you are trying to force someone to do something they don't want to do; and when you are tempted to nag, remind, or rescue inappropriately.

The best way to let go is to do something to calm down and relax. Remove yourself from the situation so that you can reflect on it from a distance. Take a walk or a soothing bath. Meditate. Read a book that inspires you. From the shelter of a calm outlook, we can usually find a peaceful way to handle a situation.

Some people confuse indifference or not caring with letting go. For example, after several verbal bouts with your teenager, out of sheer frustration, you say in a resigned tone, " Oh, go on to the party then. I don't care." This is not letting go! When you let go, you care deeply what the outcome will be. You simply know you have done your best and you have decided to trust that things will work out.

My son was having a hard time learning to tell time. I decided to help him. I created one learning tool after another. I coached and coaxed until we were both exhausted. Nothing I did worked. Finally, I decided to let go. I comforted myself with the thought that surely by the time he was thirty years old, he would be able to tell time.

A few months later my son asked for a watch for his birthday. The parenting gods smiled on me and I refrained from saying, "Why? You can't read it." Instead, I bought the watch. Later in the week, I was due to pick up my son at 3:15 p.m. I arrived at 3:17 p.m. and was greeted with, "You're late!"

Make things happen

One way I take care of myself is to figure out what I want to have happen and then to make it happen. This leads to an increase in self-confidence. There was a time when I couldn't figure out what I wanted because I was too concerned about being liked. If my husband asked what movie I'd like to see, I'd respond by asking him what he'd like to see. With my children and in other relationships, I now ask myself, "What do I want to see happen in this situation?"

For example, if my child asks to go to the movie on a Sunday afternoon, I ask myself, "What do I want?" Do I want family time or do I need time by myself or time alone with my husband? Once I know, then I negotiate accordingly with my child.

Lead a balanced life

Pay attention to these seven areas of life and keep them in balance so that you feel alive and satisfied. If you aren't successful or fulfilled in one area, it may have an adverse affect on other areas. They are:

- spiritual
- education; learning
- career; vocation
- social (family and friends, etc.)
- physical
- financial
- recreation; relaxation

Make a commitment to improve the balance where necessary. For example, if you get no exercise (a common physical problem for many of us), commit to a way of exercise that is enjoyable for you. If your finances are in disarray, take a class in budgeting.

Nurture yourself

It is important for every parent to have at least thirty minutes each day to restore energy. Finding time for yourself takes commitment, creativity, and determination. The opportunities are not always obvious. Here are some of my ideas for time alone; add your own and take time for renewal:

- Get up earlier or go to bed later than everyone else in your household.

- Use your lunch hour for time alone—walking, thinking, reading, meditating, or dreaming.

- Hire a baby sitter, or swap baby sitting with a relative or friend, for a couple of hours.

- Alternate time off with your partner, so that you both benefit.

In addition to time alone, parents need to do things that give them pleasure and nurture them, just as they do this for their children. Do things for yourself that make you feel better. These ideas might get you started; add your own to the list:

- Take bubble baths or long, hot showers that relax you. Music and candlelight can be delightful additions to the experience and raise it above the ordinary.

- Take walks, especially in the rain or snow.

- Get a professional massage.

- Listen to relaxing music or motivational tapes.

- Meditate.

- Sit or work in the garden.

- Write in your journal, putting down both the pleasant and unpleasant events of the day.

- Play a musical instrument or draw or paint or build.

A mother of three children under the age of five told me how impossible it was for her to get away alone. I told her I understood; however, I wanted her to commit to finding some way to take care of herself. When she came back to class the following week, she looked great. Everyone wanted to know what she had done.

She told us, "I used to love playing the piano, but I haven't played it since the kids were born. The day it rained last week, things were really getting out of control. I just wanted to scream. Then I remembered my commitment and sat down at the piano. It was amazing! I worked out my frustrations and I noticed that the kids got calmer, too."

The most important thing that I can tell you is to take care of yourself. If you take time for yourself, you will be ready for the constant demands that parenting places on you. Everything you are about to learn from this book will feel easier and come more naturally because you will have the energy to make changes.

2

Encourage Your Child

When children are little, they are full of confidence; they believe they can do anything; they have unlimited potential. If you were to ask a group of kindergartners, "How many of you believe you could be a great doctor, scientist, or President of the United States?" most hands would go up quickly and self-assuredly. But, ask that question of a group of teenagers and fewer than half will raise their hands. By the time we are adults, most of us have long since forgotten or given up our dreams. What happened?

Imagine your child's spirit as a brightly

glowing flame that dances and grows with each piece of fuel you feed it. Now, imagine someone pouring sand on the flame. The result? Depending on how much sand and the speed at which it is poured, the flame fades or goes out.

We dampen or put out a child's flame (spirit) by nagging, yelling, spanking, being overprotective or controlling, and using threats, guilt, shame, or punishment to correct misbehavior. Every day you have hundreds of opportunities to kindle a child's spirit, rather than dampen it. Encouragement is the way to keep your child's spirit burning brightly. Let's talk about the most important ways to do this.

Honor your child's unique self

Parents tend to spend a great deal more time trying to mold their children to be different from who they are than honoring them as they are. Everywhere I go I hear phrases such as these:

- Don't be silly.
- Be quiet.
- Stop crying.
- Shame on you.
- You're so noisy.
- You're bad.
- Don't be sad.
- You're being selfish.
- You're just like . . .
- Why can't you be like . . .

There is many an unhappy adult who is still doing (or not doing) something because of his or her parents' influence through such small criticisms that leave lasting impressions. Respect and honor your child's uniqueness. Parent and child live best together when each can fully express who they are.

Give unconditional love

Our children need unconditional love from their parents. There is no greater encouragement for a child. This love doesn't depend on some performance. It is given simply because a child is, no more and no less. There is nothing he or she has to do, no standard or parent's dream to live up to, no good grades or clean room required, to earn unconditional love. How many adults do you know who strive for love through "doing" and piling up accomplishments? These individuals probably did not experience unconditional love as children.

Unconditional love is essential in raising self-confident children who love themselves, others, and the world in which they live. Only by giving our children unconditional love are they free to be the best they can be and eventually able to encourage others to be their best.

Believe in your child

An important aspect of unconditional love is belief in your child. Encouraging words and actions flow from this faith when it is positive in outlook. Our beliefs about our children shape how we respond to them. Sometimes we're not aware of our beliefs. To find out if your beliefs about your child are positive or negative, look at the labels you apply (sometimes unconsciously) to him. Sadly for the child, labels are more often negative than positive. Here are a few I hear; add your own to the list:

- stupid
- terrible two
- lazy
- shy
- hyper
- teenager
- forgetful
- brat

Labels put children in boxes that are hard to climb out of because they limit potential. Sometimes labels are excuses, also, to continue on in the same unproductive behavior. At other times, they might seem positive ("pretty" or "genius"), but still limit a child because of our mental associations with the terms.

If you have just realized how you are limiting your child by failing to believe in her potential, throw out the labels and open your mind. Look for ways to let your "lazy" son become cooperative and active. Help your "pretty princess" learn how to do practical things that allow her to be independent. Change the label and your expectation. Your child will respond positively.

Support your child's dreams

Help your child develop her natural abilities, out of which her hopes and dreams are most likely to come. Find out what her dreams and aspirations are and support her to fulfill them. Remember that she is different from you and your belief in her has great influence on how she sees herself. Sometimes we expect children to fulfill our dreams through their actions. This is a terrible burden for a child: she is put in the precarious position of wanting to please you and wanting to fulfill her own dreams. When the two desires are incompatible, the scene is set for strife between you.

When you help children fulfill their dreams, you teach them they can accomplish what is important to them. This faith helps them maintain a healthy attitude about life. Many teenagers and adults have given up their dreams. As a result, their lives have less meaning and may be dull.

This father failed to honor his son's unique spirit, natural ability, and dream for himself:

Dad wanted his son to be a dentist, a profession that provided a secure living. The son wanted to be a musician instead. After a lot of coercion, the son reluctantly went to dental school. The other students loved him because he would put dental terminology to music and play it on the piano to help everyone memorize before exams. After he completed his degree, he gave his diploma to his father and left for Nashville to pursue a career in music.

For this son, pleasing Dad was important, and fortunately he didn't give up his own dream. However, Dad and he would have had a much better relationship if Dad had more readily accepted his son's interest in music.

Parents can support their children's dreams in various ways, according to their emotional and material resources. Here is a dad who did so on a grand scale:

A teenager had a dream of playing hockey in the Olympic Games. His father, who also had a passion for hockey, bought a skating rink so that the family could combine making a living and supporting the son's dream. Dad hired a coach, who developed a hockey team for his son to play on.

You can honor your child's dream by changing your attitude, easier for many of us than buying a skating rink.

A father had a son who was not doing very well academically. Dad noticed, however, that his son excelled in gymnastics. So, instead of pushing the child in his studies, Dad concentrated on helping him feel successful in athletics. He did not ignore his son's studies, but he focused on what the child did well and encouraged him to pursue his dream.

Show that you believe in your child and support her by going to her school events and teacher conferences, recitals, games, and other activities and by recognizing all areas into which she puts effort. Many adults complain that their parents were so busy working that they never had time to pay attention to the important events in their children's lives. Be careful not to let your child's growing years slip by without encouraging her every chance you get. Keep that flame glowing.

Genuine Encounter Moments (GEMS)

Dorothy Briggs, author of *Your Child's Self-Esteem,* describes a genuine encounter moment as focused attention. Such attention carries a special intensity born of direct, personal involvement with your child. "Many parents are with their children physically, but mentally their focus is elsewhere. Togetherness without genuine encounter is not togetherness at all," she writes.

When your child comes to you to tell you something, you have choices: 1) ignore her, 2) pretend to listen, or 3) listen attentively. When you listen attentively, you are having a Genuine Encounter Moment. Your child gets 100% of your attention; you're not thinking about what to have for dinner or the argument with your spouse. GEM's work best when you are at the child's level, looking directly into her eyes, touching her, and trying to feel what she's feeling. GEM's are not times for lectures or advice or lessons. They are times for heart to heart, not head to head, communication.

It isn't humanly possible for every conversation with your child to be a GEM. However, if you can arrange to have several GEM's each day, you'll see a marked improvement in your relationship.

The National Family Institute reports that "the average child in America receives only 12.5 minutes per day in communication with his parents. Of that time, 8.5 minutes are spent with the parent in correcting, criticizing, or arguing. This leaves only 4 minutes per day for the instruction of values, morals, ethics, attitudes, and self-esteem."

GEM's help your child feel acknowledged, important, cared for, and valuable. When children get this kind of attention, they have little need to use misbehavior in order to get attention.

Teach your child to use positive self-talk

Self-talk is the voice inside your head that tells you how you're doing. The messages you give your children at a young age often become their self-talk as they grow. Encouragement results in positive self-talk and high self-esteem.

Many adults have a great deal of trouble getting rid of negative self-talk heard when they were children. Your aim is to replace self-talk like "I can't," "I don't know how," "I'm shy," and so on with "I can," "I will learn," "I can talk to one person," and other positive, hopeful messages in the child's mind.

Be careful what messages you give your child and be aware of how he might interpret what you say. For example, one mother frequently and lovingly called her youngest child "baby." Later, she found out the term made her child feel small and powerless, definitely not what she had intended! Check it out with your child by asking, "How do you feel when I say . . . ?"

Tone of voice

Your tone of voice also influences how your child receives your message. Keep a light, nonjudgmental tone to your voice. Children feel demeaned when you use baby talk. Use big words and let them ask you what they mean. Talk as if you were talking to one of your adult friends. Speak respectfully, which helps your child feel important and competent.

Honor your child's intentions

When you speak to her about misbehavior, include words that show you understand what her true intention is. For example, if your daughter pesters the cat, you might say, "You're hurting the cat. I know that is not what you intend because you're usually loving to him. Is there something you want to talk about?" If you say, "Stop hurting the cat," her behavior is likely to be directed toward a new victim or continue in some other way.

Usually children misbehave unconsciously. When you bring their mistake to their attention in a loving way and tone, they can look at their behavior and decide what to do about it without getting hung up on discouraging self-talk ("I'm bad.").

Promote internal motivation

Emphasize the joy of doing instead of out doing. Help your child focus on how she feels about her good grades, rather than wondering about what someone else will think of them. Say, "It looks like you really like to learn," or "That must make you feel good." You want her good feeling to come from within her.

If a child feels she is okay only as long as she has someone else's approval, she develops the idea that other people's opinions are more important than her own. This belief will backfire when she becomes subject to peer pressure, and it makes her an easy target for inappropriate sexual activity, drugs, gangs, and physical abuse.

Express affection

A major human need is for physical contact with others. Without it, children fail to thrive. Showing your love for your child through physical expression is a powerful way to offer encouragement. Let your entire body express the positive feelings you have for your child. Hold a small child on your lap to read or talk or just be. Stoop down to your child's level and look at her. Move close to her. Don't yell at her from across the room or the yard. Put your arm around her or on her shoulder. If she's a pre-teen or teenager who doesn't want much physical contact, sit near her or allow her to lean over your shoulder. Smile at her to show her you accept and appreciate her. These suggestions might seem unnecessary, but it's amazing how little time we take to do these simple things that offer encouragement and can turn a child around.

Respect your child's boundaries

Some parents are confused about appropriate expression of physical affection, especially now with so many reports about sexual abuse in the news. The guidelines are the following:

- Do only that which is appropriate for your child's age,
- Respects him or her,
- Does not cause bad feelings, and
- Is acceptable to the child.

It is very important for children's growth and self-esteem to respect their physical and emotional boundaries. When adults don't respect these boundaries, children do not learn to put limits on how other people treat them. They may find it difficult to say "No!" to strangers, to people wanting sexual favors, or to others who wish to take advantage of them in some way. Boys are as vulnerable as girls, though we hear more often about abuse to girls.

Boundary invasions include the following:

- Entering an older child's bathroom or bedroom without knocking and asking permission

- Forcing affection that the child doesn't want (including kisses and hugs from relatives)

- Cleaning up an older child's room without permission

- Forcing food on a child

- Forcing medicine on a child

- Borrowing money or possessions without permission

- Telling the child's confidences to others without permission (including the other parent)

- Making the child tell private thoughts or give information

- Continuing to tickle or roughhouse when the child wants to stop

- Reading an older child's mail, diary, or class papers without permission

Even when it is necessary for a child's health and safety to do some things, such as give medicine, enter a room, or read something, we can do so respectfully and give advance notice.

Sometimes parents unwittingly disrespect a boundary, especially when the child is young.

Three-year-old James was out with his parents and needed to change his clothes. He didn't want people to see him but there was no place that was private. His dad tried to talk him out of his need for privacy since he was only three. Luckily, Dad realized that he was undermining the lessons he'd been teaching his son about personal safety. He provided a large towel behind which James could change.

A woman remembers when she broke her leg as a child and the doctors cut off her jeans and underpants in order to work on her leg. They acted without explaining why or asking her permission to take off her clothes. To this day she recalls how scared and violated she felt.

It may be hard to tell if a child is really enjoying physical affection, like being tickled or kissed. My children and I have developed a signal we use to indicate when we've had enough. When the tickled person says, "Please stop," the tickler does so immediately. We respect one another's physical and emotional boundaries. Children feel empowered when adults and other children respect their boundaries.

Order and Routine

The establishment of order and routine in your home develops a sense of security for your children. Routines give the child something he can count on. Think of how unsafe and insecure we adults would feel if just one thing in our daily lives changed—we could drive on either side of the road whenever we felt like it. It's important for children to know, to some degree, what they can expect, too. They need this stability as a springboard for confidence. Children who don't have order and routine are too often reeling from the last thing that happened to them. They stand little chance of developing a strong foundation of self-confidence.

Bedtime seems to be a particularly difficult time for most parents and one that can go much more smoothly with a routine. Everyone is usually tired and stressed by the end of the day, which only makes matters worse. I have chosen to demonstrate how routine can be established, in general, through use of bedtime as the specific example.

Time for bed

"Zachary, time for bed," announces Mom. "No!" two-year-old Zachary yelps, running toward the playroom. Mother follows close behind, pleading, "It's time for bed, honey. C'mon, now." "No, Mommy, no!" squeals Zachary, as Mother swoops down to pick him up. Zachary's body stiffens, his back arches, and he begins wildly kicking his feet in order to free himself of her tightening grip.

"Stop it! You're going to bed, NOW!" Mother declares, determined to get her struggling child to bed. Zachary begins to cry loudly as Mother, as exasperated as she can be, pulls off his clothes for his bath. This emotional and physical power struggle continues through bath, pajamas, tooth brushing, and abruptly ends with a token goodnight kiss.

Exhausted and frustrated, Mother sags down the stairs hoping for some peace and quiet, only to hear, "Mommy, drink. Me go potty!" Mother angrily takes Zachary a glass of water and makes a quick trip to the bathroom with him. She sets him on his bed and says through clenched teeth, "Don't let me hear another peep out of you. Good night!"

Mother stomps down the stairs after slamming Zachary's door. Zachary is left huddled on his bed, crying into his pillow, and Mother feels guilty and frustrated.

Now, look at this same scene through Zachary's eyes. Because of our myopic, parental viewpoint, we miss the opportunity to understand how our child sees it.

Imagine that you are in the middle of a good book and your spouse says, "It's time for bed." In spite of your response, "No,

I'm not ready just yet," he (or she) helps you unwillingly up the stairs, your clothes are removed, and you're forced to take a bath. Consider how you feel. Do you feel disrespected, violated, angry, or controlled? You may be thinking, "Yes, but a two-year-old doesn't feel this way – it's not the same, he's not an adult. Besides, I'm the parent." True, the child is not yet an adult. However, he is a person, with feelings. He's at an important growth stage: he wants independence and is experimenting with how to have his choices be known and honored.

Many times, going to bed is not the issue; he may be tired and ready for bed. Yet the parent's command makes him feel controlled. Don't we adults feel that way, too, when we are "commanded" in the same way? We naturally want control over ourselves and what happens to us. As Mother continues to overpower Zachary, he feels unloved and rejected.

Bedtime can be a special time for closeness between parents and children. It is natural for us to desire closeness or connectedness before going to sleep. Often, however, parents have overburdened themselves during the day. They're eager to get the child in bed as soon as possible so they can have some quiet time for themselves. The child is likely to feel that his parents are trying to "get rid of him." Our children show that they haven't had enough closeness by repeatedly demanding drinks and potty breaks.

What does your child really want?
- To declare his independence or sense of self
- To feel close or connected with his parents
- To feel a sense of control over what happens to him
- To feel respected and heard

How can you, as a parent, give your child what he wants and needs and still have him go to bed in a timely manner?

Respect your own needs. Take care of yourself during the day so that you're not feeling hassled and frazzled at your child's bedtime. Set your child's bedtime for an hour that allows you some solitude or "couple time" with your partner after your child is tucked into bed and has gone to sleep.

Whenever possible, have both parents be a part of the bedtime ritual. Bedtime is more fun and less of a burden when both parents participate.

Start your bedtime ritual forty-five minutes to one hour before your child's actual bedtime hour to avoid unnecessary stress and struggle. This process should be a winding down time. In other words, eliminate activities that would excite the child, such as roughhousing or tickling.

Respect his sense of time by telling him that bedtime is in fifteen minutes, allowing him to complete a particular activity before his actual bedtime hour.

Offer choices instead of orders. Your child will have a feeling of control over what happens to him when you give him choices. For example, you might say, "Do you want your dad to help you with your bath or me?" or, "Do you want to sleep with your gorilla or your kitty?"

Create a bedtime ritual with your child's help and advice. For example, read a story, snuggle, say a prayer, give a hug and two kisses, and leave the room singing a song. The routine needs to have a quality of sameness – the same order or the same song for young children–in order to provide a sense of security.

Create closeness. For example, talk about "Remember when," such as, "Remember when we went camping and that raccoon got into our food stash?" or, "I remember when you were a little baby and loved to have your tummy rubbed." These conversations set the stage for peaceful sleep without bad dreams.

Say three things that you love about each other. Start each statement with, "What I love about you is . . . " and complete it with a specific thing you love. You might say, "What I love about you is the way your singing can lift my spirits."

Ask the following questions which allow your child to share more about himself, "What was the best thing that happened to you today?" and "What was the worst thing that happened today?"

Some children may talk more freely with the lights out. Try to discover what most encourages your child to communicate with you.

After you have completed your bedtime routine, leave your child's room. Explain once when you start this new bedtime routine, "If you come out of your room for any reason other than emergency, I will lovingly guide or carry you back to your room. I will not talk to you after saying good night and closing your bedroom door."

It's important that you do not talk to your child after the bedtime routine is complete. If you continue to talk with your child, you are more likely to get into a verbal power struggle. You may have to guide your child back to his room several times, particularly at the beginning because children will test their parents. However, as the week progresses, bedtime will become more pleasant for both you and your child.

You can make bedtime a time of nurturing, closeness, shared communication, and fun. By involving your children in the decision-making process and spending this special time with them, they will feel valued and respected.

When you have order and routine, your child feels secure because he learns he can depend on certain events consistently occurring.

Filter your child's experiences

One of our jobs as a parent is to filter out experiences that would overwhelm our children. Among these are abuse of any kind, physical danger, or experiences simply too complex for the child's level and stage of development. However, it is equally important that we allow challenging experiences into our child's life. Through these he learns to be self-confident. The more often a child copes successfully with challenges, the greater his self-confidence and skills grow.

The child in this story faces both an unreasonable experience for her age and a reasonable one. Her mother thoughtfully filters the outcomes of each to maximize her daughter's learning.

On the day of her departure for her grandparents' house, twelve-year-old Melissa left her plane ticket on the dresser in her bedroom. Mom happened to see it laying there. She considered the idea of saying nothing, but she felt this natural consequence of a missed plane would be too disappointing for Melissa. So Mom picked up the ticket and handed it to Melissa without saying anything. Melissa sheepishly took the ticket and placed it on the dashboard of the car.

As they walked into the airport, Mom noticed that Melissa had again forgotten the ticket. At this point, Mom realized they were early and would have time to deal with the natural consequence of the forgotten ticket, so she said nothing. Halfway to the ticket counter, Melissa gasped, "Oh, my gosh, I forgot my ticket again!" Without critical words or looks, Mom handed the car keys to Melissa, who ran back and retrieved her ticket from the car.

Use mistakes to encourage your child

Mistakes are a fact of life; we all make them, often. Take advantage of this readily available source of encouragement. When your child makes a mistake, don't scold him. His fear of your disapproval will cause him to cover up mistakes, lie, or blame others for his actions. He may also become fearful of taking risks in life.

It's okay to make mistakes—few of them are fatal—and we learn a great deal about what to do differently next time. Here are five suggestions that minimize the mistake itself and maximize encouragement of your child.

1. **Emphasize what the child can do next time.** Too much concern with what has already happened only encourages excuses and defensiveness from your child. Help your child figure out what to do differently the next time and teach him a new skill if he needs one.

Mistakes happen. How could you hold the carton so you won't spill the milk next time?"

2. **Separate the deed from the doer.** Reassure your child that you love her, but that you're unwilling to accept misbehavior.

   "I love you and I don't like what you're doing right now."

3. **Give your child another chance.** This shows your child you have faith in his ability to improve.

   "You made a mess while eating in the family room yesterday. You may not eat there today, but you can try again tomorrow."

4. **Show your child what to do.** Usually we tell a child what to do. Sometimes this frustrates both parent and child. Many children learn best when adults show them what they want and then ask the child to do the same. Pay attention to your child's preferred learning style. Try to use all three major learning styles each time you teach a new skill: visual (seeing), auditory (listening), and kinesthetic (doing, hands-on).

   "Watch how I pour the cereal into the bowl, and then how I pour the milk slowly. See? That way you don't spill any."

5. **Ask questions.** Ask questions that encourage your child to figure things out on his own. Ask in a loving, accepting voice, "What did you learn from that? What will you do differently next time? What would happen if . . . ?" Your child will learn more when he thinks of his own solutions than when he listens to yours. This is especially true of teenagers. Questions guide children in a way that prevents them from failing. Consequently, their feelings of self-reliance increase.

We don't enjoy seeing children fail, so our natural inclination is to offer them every possible help they might need. They sense our doubt about their ability to complete things "correctly" without our help. Seek the balance between doing everything for your child on the one hand and letting him suffer repeated failure on the other. Your goal is to encourage him to solve problems himself and to seek help when he needs it.

Teach children to repair mistakes

Children need to learn to take responsibility for their mistakes. It is important for them to learn how to make amends for a mistake that harms someone or someone's property. Parents can teach by modeling the behavior and by asking questions. If you bump into a car in the parking lot and the owner is not around to demand repair of the mistake, you can bet that your children will take note of whether you leave your name and telephone number or whether you escape as quickly as possible, hoping no one noticed.

A father allowed his children to use his tools to do a project. They got spots of paint on the handles of his tools. The father asked them what they might do to repair their mistake. The kids asked their dad if they could paint all the handles silver.

A child went home after school with a friend without calling her mother first to let her know where she'd be. Mother went to school to pick up her daughter and couldn't find her. The daughter decided that since she had made her mother drive out of her way by not calling her and had taken up Mother's time unnecessarily, she would do one of her mother's chores to make up for her error.

It is important that the person who makes the mistake determine how to make up for it. What is decided has to be acceptable to the person who was inconvenienced. Your goal is for your child to learn to think about repairing mistakes on her own. She may need your help to remember if she is young or the skill is new to her.

Common parent misbehaviors

Parents who use these methods to control their children's behavior fail to encourage their children to be all they can be. Check off any you use and work consciously to throw them out of your parenting tool box.

Hassle over minor issues

Choose only the most important issues to work on so you don't overwhelm your child. Keep the work lighthearted, if possible.

My husband likes a tidy house. After meeting with great resistance from the rest of us, he came up with a delightful way to get our cooperation. Every night before bed we all pick up for ten minutes. My husband sets the timer and puts on lively music, and we all dash around picking as much as we can. When the timer goes off, we stop. We celebrate what we accomplished.

Humiliation

This technique might get the behavior you wish at the moment, but you lay the groundwork for vengeance and mistrust. It is especially harmful when you use it in front of your child's friends. Avoid saying things like, "If you don't stop wetting your pants, I'm going to make you wear a diaper to school!" or, "You're never on time. Tell your friends to go home and get in the house right now."

Criticism

The average child receives 432 negative comments per day versus 32 positive ones. Scary thought, isn't it? Avoid criticism and disapproval. Respond to your child in a way that helps him feel encouraged. Give him constructive messages.

A school principal requires that teachers send five children to his office for good behavior before they can send one for misbehavior. His policy has changed the way his teachers think about their students.

Overuse of "No" and "Don't"

It's discouraging for children to hear these two words often. Many times we say them over things that don't really matter. Children will respond more cooperatively if you tell them two things they can do instead. Say, "Walls are not for coloring on. You may color on this paper or on the sidewalk behind the house." Or, "Yes, I'll take you to the mall as soon as you've done your chores."

Comparison/competition

Comparison of one person to another breeds competition. Competition pits person against person and makes each feel like he has to be better than the other. This is a hopeless situation because there will always be one who can do something better than another.

The child who is taught cooperation instead of competition will be happiest and have the versatility to survive in our world. A person who must always try to prove himself will never be at peace.

Overprotection

When parents overprotect children, they send the message that life is dangerous and children can't handle it. Children need suitable opportunities to struggle with figuring out how to deal with the challenges they face. Through struggling, they learn skills and gain confidence in their abilities to take care of themselves.

I invited a friend's eight-year-old son to go swimming with my son. Todd had chronic ear infections and had to use ear plugs. He asked me to put them in for him, as his mother always did. I smiled and touched his shoulder and said, "I think you can figure out how to do it."

As he whined and complained, I stood silent. Finally, he began to struggle with the ear plugs. After dropping them, putting them in upside down, and so on, he at last succeeded. The pride he obviously felt was a wonder to see!

Failure to parent with the end in mind

Parents have the responsibility to prepare their children for adulthood. Some techniques, such as overpowering children, looking for the expedient solution that solves a problem in the short run but fails to help the child learn, giving insufficient time or having too little patience cause problems for children that they must deal with in adulthood. As you parent your child, ask yourself, "What will my child learn from this discipline? Will it help him develop characteristics he needs as an adult?"

Failure to learn from our children

We expect our children to learn from us, because we are the adults. However, there is no reason why parents can't learn from their children, too, once they keep an open mind and really observe what their children do well.

Mom said to seven-year-old Judy, "It's really neat how you go into your room when you're mad. When you come back out, you're ready to talk." Judy looked at Mom strangely and said, "Yeah, Mom."

A couple of weeks later, Mom and Dad were having a huge fight. Judy cautiously approached Mom and said, "Sometimes when I'm mad, I go to my room and think happy thoughts. Then it's not so bad when I come out." Mom and Dad caught each other's eyes and grinned sheepishly. They stopped fighting, and both thought of a different way to handle angry situations.

Use encouragement genuinely

Children can tell if their parents' encouragement is genuine or phony. Insincere encouragement is manipulative. Ask yourself, "Does what I say empower my child or is it an attempt to control or alter her behavior? Do I say this to get my child to be the way I want her to be or to honor who she already is?"

An elementary teacher once called Rudolf Dreikurs, M.D., the well-known psychiatrist, into her classroom. She began to complain to Dr. Dreikurs about a child's poor handwriting, in front of the child. "Look at this mess. Have you ever seen such horrible penmanship? You can't read a thing on this whole paper!"

Dr. Dreikurs studied the paper and then smiled at the child. "I don't know . . . that's a pretty nicely shaped 'O' right there," he said, *pointing at the only legible letter on the page. His encouraging comment provided the motivation for the child to work on his penmanship, whereas all the teacher's criticism had not.*

When you tell a child what he or she has done well—be it the end result or simply the effort that went into the activity, regardless of the result—you're using a very effective teaching method. On the other hand, when you try to motivate a child with critical or discouraging words, she's likely to give up or become defensive. Hold in the front of your mind your goal for your child: an adult who is healthy, self-confident, self-reliant, and cooperative.

THE FAMILY ENCOURAGEMENT FEAST

An encouragement feast can be held at the dinner table, family meetings, in the car, or spontaneously anywhere, anytime. This is a way to focus on what you love about each other. At first, you may feel awkward if you're not accustomed to complimenting one another in your family. That's okay. Practice will get you over that self-consciousness. The pleasure you see on the faces around you will keep you practicing.

Begin by putting a family member in the middle of a circle or at the head of the table, or in some other spot of honor. Hold her or his hands. Instruct each member of the family to say, "What I love about you is . . ." When each person has had a turn, the honored person says what he or she loves about himself or herself and then chooses the next family member to be in the place of honor. This continues until each person has had a turn. The closeness and warm, positive feelings make this the best family game ever!

3

Three Parenting Styles

Most parents use one of three common parenting styles or, perhaps, a blend of two or three. It is helpful here to define these three styles so that we can determine what form of discipline we use most often, and decide if we wish to continue with that method or exchange it for something more effective and encouraging to our child. The parenting styles I refer to are autocratic (sometimes called authoritarian), permissive, and democratic.

Autocratic parenting

Jason's report card has a D on it. His dad sees it and yells, "No son of mine is going to get D's on his report card! You're grounded for two weeks. Now get in your room and study!"

Autocratic parents view children and situations as bad or wrong. They use force as the discipline tool to manipulate their child to do what they want. Force includes guilt, threats, punishment, grounding, spanking, sarcasm, criticism, intimidation, humiliation, withdrawal of love, commands (not related to immediate safety), bribes, and other attempts to control or make children (or anyone) do something against their will. All of these methods dampen the child's spirit, self-esteem, and self-confidence.

Force, or coercive power, motivates through fear instead of love. Fear makes children feel they are not "good enough." A moment's reflection will remind you of times when you have felt the effect of coercive power in your adult life—you understand how destructive it can be.

Fear used as a motivator causes children to protect themselves by lying and blaming others. Fear leads to competition, fighting, separation from others, and hostility. Fear of punishment also causes children to give up who they are to become what someone else wants them to be or to rebel against what someone else wants. The child's behavior is controlled by an outside source (parent, teacher), rather than by the child's own sense of what is right or wrong. Punishment doesn't develop self-responsibility in a child, nor does it show him how to develop his own moral standards. Instead, children often try to "get away with" misbehavior.

Illusion of effectiveness

Coercive force may immediately cause your child to stop the behavior you object to; however, its effectiveness is only an illusion. The technique "works" for the moment, but doesn't promote the learning you wish to see in the long run.

When you use punishment, the child either becomes compliant or resistant and revengeful. After being punished, a child often focuses on getting even with you (or any other authority figure), rather than thinking about the consequences of his inappropriate behavior and what he learned from his behavior. Children usually respond to coercion in an equally coercive manner by sulking, being uncooperative, picking on younger siblings or pets, getting bad grades at school, destroying his own property or yours, running away from home, and "forgetting" to do chores. The list of negative reactions is as long as children are creative. As parents, one response to such behavior is more coercion, resulting in revengeful, hostile, stressful, blaming, uncooperative, disrespectful behavior from our children. Everyone's self-concept is damaged; there is much tension and a lack of respect and cooperation. We say and do things we wish we could edit out of our lives.

Obedience versus responsibility

A confusion many parents have is the distinction between obedi-ence and responsibility. On rare occasions, children must be obedient for their own safety. A small child must stop at the curb, get away from the hot stove, or stay back from a body of water. Beyond issues of safety, it is more important that children learn to be responsible to the demands of the situation than obedient to an authority figure. By this statement, I mean that children need to learn to think about situations and use their reasoning ability to arrive at the best course of action. This takes problem-solving abil-ity, brainstorming (creativity), and awareness of feelings. If you demand blind obedience from your child, you are limiting her abil-ity to learn how to act responsibly.

Parents who use force do so mostly because that's how they themselves were parented. Other parents use it when they are anx-ious about some stress in their own life: a conflict with a spouse or at work, too little time for themselves, or illness. There are many possible reasons. If a child defies you at such a time, you feel even more powerless, and the quick fix of a swat or grounding seems the right way. Yet other parents use force because they believe children must be "taught a lesson" or punished in order for them to learn new ways of behaving.

Check in with yourself the next time you punish your child with force. Ask yourself these questions:

- Am I angry, do I want to hurt back, do I feel powerless?

- Do I want my child to do what I ask in order to a) be a better person, or b) get him to obey me?

- Do I want to control my child, or would I rather teach him to control himself?

- Am I using fear or love to motivate my child?

- What do I want my child to learn right now?

- How can I teach what I want him to learn without using force (being coercive)?

Someday in the future, the use of spanking and other physical force as discipline will be as archaic as women not being allowed to vote or black people being forced to sit in the back of the bus.

REASONS FOR AVOIDING PHYSICAL FORCE TO DISCIPLINE CHILDREN

(Adapted from *Spare the Rod* by Phil E. Quinn)

1. Use of physical force (corporal punishment) says fear, pain, intimidation, and violence are acceptable methods of resolving conflicts between people, no matter what their age.

2. Physical force is unnecessary. There are many nonviolent disciplinary alternatives which are more effective and pose no risk or harm to children.

3. Physical force confuses discipline with punishment. Discipline is used to teach, while punishment is used for purposes of control and retribution. Young children do not commit crimes that require punishment. Their mistakes call for discipline, that is, teaching more appropriate response.

4. Physical force inhibits better means of communication and problem solving. People who use it make little effort to learn nonviolent ways.

5. Physical force confuses love and violence. Children get the impression that violence can be an expression of love. True love is expressed in much healthier, nonviolent ways.

6. Physical force only controls the symptom of a problem. It does not address and, in fact, makes worse the cause of the problem.

7. Physical force is dangerous. It can escalate into battering and sometimes results in death. It is very likely to result in physical, mental, spiritual, or emotional harm.

8. Research has shown that physical force increases aggressiveness in children and contributes to vandalism in schools and on the streets. Violence leads to more violence.

9. Physical force reduces a child's ability to concentrate, making it harder for her to learn.

10. Physical force denies your child a right to equal protection under the law—a right guaranteed to all citizens in the United States in Section I of the Fourteenth Amendment to the Constitution of the United States.

Rewards

Dad sees the D on Jason's report card. He says, "If you bring that grade up to a B, I'll give you $10.00."

Love given only as a reward and material rewards used to bait or bribe children to get them to behave in a certain way invariably backfire. Rewards can be just as controlling as punishment. Children who receive rewards are also dependent on the parent or some other authority figure for the will to accomplish a task. The success of rewards must be judged by whether or not there is a lasting effect on the child's behavior. However, rewards, in and of themselves, do not change behavior. Many parents are confused about this. As with punishment, if the person giving the reward is not around, the child has no motivation internally to behave as you want her to. Another problem is that the rewards may need to get bigger or better in order for them to change short-term behavior.

Material rewards change the reason your child does something and the attitude with which he does it. If you ask your child to do things with a reward attached to the request, your child begins to focus on how to get more and better rewards. He does not develop an inner sense of accomplishment and self-satisfaction, which ultimately should become the guiding force behind effort.

Rewards can interfere with the development of a sense of self-worth. Children may interpret being rewarded to mean they don't need to do anything until there is something in it for them. We know that we often feel the most worthwhile when we do something for someone else and expect nothing in return. Our culture, though, emphasizes things as the source of good feeling, and children are influenced by this emphasis. There is more to life than "What's in it for me?" In fact, developing a feeling of self-worth is essential to good mental health. True giving is enormously good for the human soul. If you rely on rewards to teach children how you want them to behave, you deny them the opportunity to learn to act from an internal source of motivation and strength.

Perhaps you recall the incident in which people were outraged at a gas station attendant. On the street in front of the gas station, a man's car caught on fire. Flames engulfed the dashboard. The driver was frantically trying to put the fire out with his coat. The gas station attendant arrived on the scene with a fire extinguisher and said to the driver, "For twenty dollars I'll let you use my fire extinguisher."

The point I wish to make is that you want your child to behave appropriately for many reasons other than what material goods she expects to receive as a result.

Most people in our society work for a reward—a paycheck. Were it not for that paycheck, many adults would not do the work they do. For too many, the paycheck is the only incentive they have for going to their jobs. The paycheck does allow them to support themselves and their families, and therefore may be seen to have value for a higher good than just material things. It is a well-known fact, however, that people who do work that gives them satisfaction beyond the money they receive are happier, healthier, and more productive than those who don't like the work they do. That's because satisfying work gives a person a feeling of self-worth and internal satisfaction—the attributes we parents wish to develop in our children.

Permissive parenting

Jason shows Dad the D on his report card. Dad says, "It's okay, Son. You'll do better next time."

If rewards and punishments aren't the ways to discipline children, does that mean we should let them do whatever they wish? Should we make no effort to teach them how to behave and be responsible?

Permissive parenting may take the form of not caring about a child's grades, or who her friends are, or where she is, or what time she gets home, or giving in when the situation calls for firmness. Permissiveness makes the child feel like you don't care, even when you do, and, as a result, she may seek care and concern from other people. There are many teenage girls who are so hungry for affection that they end up pregnant. What they want, even though they seem to want you to think otherwise from their rebellion, is obvious guidance, limits, and affection.

Being permissive and indulgent with children causes them to disrespect the parents and also themselves. When you allow your child to take advantage of you, it tears away at her own self-esteem. Children really do not like to be permitted to misbehave. Sometimes we parents are permissive because we don't want to deal with conflict. If we let our child do what he wants, we avoid conflict at that moment, but in the long run we create a bigger problem and we'll have to deal with it later.

Permissive parents also do not teach their children the skills they need to live a fulfilled life. Children's mistakes provide opportunities for many lessons on how to do things differently. If you let these mistakes go unnoticed or do not deal with them directly, you deprive your child of valuable information. Such disregard may not be your intention, but it is the effect of permissive parenting.

The recorded message from the high school told Mom that her fifteen-year-old daughter Jessica had missed five days of school. When Mom quizzed Jessica about this message, her daughter told her that the student taking attendance had made a mistake; there was no problem. Mom was relieved to hear this because she couldn't imagine smart, responsible Jessica skipping class.

Some time later Jessica seemed tired and grouchy most of the time. When her mom questioned her about her health, Jessica assured Mom that she was studying a lot and was just tired. Mom felt uneasy, but didn't want to give her daughter the message that she didn't trust her, so she said nothing more.

Over time, Jessica became rebellious, uncooperative, and argumentative. The calls from the school automated messenger became more frequent, though Jessica's grades were still B's. Life at home was very unpleasant, with Mom alternately asking what was going on or thinking the problems would disappear when Jessica outgrew this "stage." Then one day Jessica told her mom that she was pregnant and had not been going to school much for some time.

This mother has a permissive parenting approach (she does not set clear limits and strives to avoid conflict). She is not effective or assertive enough in investigating the facts behind Jessica's symptoms. Even though she loves her daughter, she fails to be the strong, involved parent this child needs in her teen years.

Democratic parenting

Jason shows Dad the D on his report card. Dad asks, "How do you feel about the D?"

"Not so good," replies Jason.

"Yeah, I'll bet that was discouraging." [Pause] "What would you like that grade to be?" Dad asks inquisitively.

"I hate fractions," pouts Jason. "They're stupid!"

"How can I help?" offers Dad.

"I don't know," Jason responds hopelessly.

"How about if I help you build that skate board ramp you've been wanting to build? That will give you some practice with those tough fractions," proposes Dad.

"Wow, when can we get started?" questions Jason.

You can see right away that democratic parenting takes more effort initially. Democratic parenting is based on the use of authentic power. It does not judge a child as wrong or bad, but allows you to unite or bond with your child. Through the use of authentic power you seek to understand rather than judge, to love unconditionally, to build positive self-concepts, and to make sure everyone wins. When parents use authentic power, they empower others. They motivate children by paying attention to feelings, needs, and desires. They help children develop control from inside themselves, maintained by the child's own set of internalized values. The child learns self-responsibility and behaves in ways that he feels are right for him. Children learn to listen quietly for inner guidance. Use of authentic power also teaches children that they are their own source of happiness. Children parented in this way experience closeness, respect, cooperation, joy, and awareness.

Mutual respect is a major part of democratic parenting. If your child does not feel respected by you, it's unlikely that he'll respond to your attempts to win his cooperation. Respect from your child can no longer be demanded or expected in our present time, it must be earned. The best way to get children to respect your rights is to respect theirs. For instance, if you want your child to knock on your door before entering your bedroom, then show him respect by knocking before entering his room.

It takes careful thought to parent in a democratic way, as this story demonstrates:

I drove four tiring hours to visit my stepdaughters. My husband and son Tyler had driven down before me to meet the girls. As I drove up, my husband and one of his daughters were getting out of the van, on their way to the house. I hugged them both and asked, "Where's Tyler?" They told me he was still in the van. I went to the van to give him a hug, too, and was greeted with, "Why did you hug her first?"

I said, "Sounds like you need someone to hold you and love you." Tyler said despondently, "Yeah, they don't like me; I hate it here." I affirmed, "When you're at home, you get Brian all to yourself. But when you come here, you not only have to share him but it also feels like the girls don't like you. Sometimes I feel that way, too." Tyler was somewhat relieved that he wasn't alone, "You do?" he asked.

I asked, "Why do you think they may have a hard time accepting us?" Tyler responded, "Because they might feel like we take their daddy away." "Probably," I agreed, as I held him closely. He stayed in my arms for a few moments and then said, "Okay, let's go inside."

Consider how this story might have turned out if I had used coercive force (as sometimes happens when I'm not feeling encouraged). I might have responded in this way:

"Why didn't you hug me first?" demands Tyler. "Because I didn't know you were still in the van. Now, hurry up, we've got to go inside," I answer sternly. Tyler says, "I don't want to go in. They don't like me." "Tyler, get your shoes on and let's go," I demand. "I'm not going in, and you can't make me!" Tyler asserts. Exasperated, I say, "Fine, just stay in

the van! I'm going in," leaving both of us feeling angry and unloved.

It is so easy to use coercive force because that's how most of us were parented. Yet, it seldom gives us the satisfaction that we're all seeking in our relationships.

How to become a democratic parent

Here are some tips to help you convert coercive force into authentic power:

1. When in doubt about what to do, back off. Don't force the issue. Admit to yourself that coercive force is not going to get the results you desire: closeness and cooperation.

2. Realize that your child is not "bad" and has not done something "wrong." He simply is, just like you are. When you misbehave, it's not because you're bad or wrong, but because you aren't getting a need met. Give your child the same respect for his needs that you want for yours.

3. Ask yourself, "How would I have liked my parent to have handled a situation like this one when I was young?"

4. Use the positive alternatives to coercive force that are discussed in this book. Brainstorm solutions with your spouse or co-workers. Watch other parents discipline their children and watch their children's reactions.

5. Try one positive alternative and acknowledge yourself if you were successful with your child. If you fail to get the result you want, ask yourself what you would do differently next time. Keep trying.

6. Attend parenting classes, read personal growth books, or participate in some type of counseling so that you can move toward loving yourself, your child, your spouse, and others in your life unconditionally.

7. Do not discourage yourself if you don't succeed in parenting

in a new way immediately. Most of us need practice before we can change our ways. Some things are easy to do right away, and some take a lot of practice. If you discourage yourself, you're likely to give up.

Some people feel awkward using authentic power (what democratic parenting is made of) at first because it is new and, like stiff, new shoes, doesn't feel good yet. If you had the task of pressing eighty-eight levers at prescribed intervals at a certain speed and, at any given time, you had to switch to a different set of levers using a different speed, could you do it? What I just described is the act of playing the piano. To play the piano well takes practice.

The same is true with these parenting techniques. They take practice and persistence. At first, you may feel uncomfortable, or you may find they don't work the way you expected. With patience and practice, you will become a more confident parent. Remember to be gentle with yourself when you make mistakes. Soon you'll be on the verge of doing something coercive and you'll catch yourself right before you do it. That's success!

Remember the goal of discipline

When a parent disciplines a child, her goal is to teach her child to be self-responsible and to act in ways that get positive results, whether an authority figure is present or not. Discipline should increase a child's awareness of her choices; these choices can make her happy or unhappy. Control over behavior thus becomes internal and contributes to the child's self-esteem.

Children misbehave when they feel discouraged or powerless. When you use discipline methods that overpower or make them feel bad about themselves (autocratic parenting), you lower their self-esteem. It doesn't make sense to punish a child who already feels bad about herself by heaping more discouragement onto her.

When you do nothing, or are ineffective in teaching the child new behavior skills, you likewise contribute to the child's feeling of discouragement and powerlessness (permissive parenting).

Parental values

Just as we often raise our children as we were raised by our parents, so we often live by the values our parents hold. Unless we consciously choose our values, most of us unconsciously accept the values of our parents and the society in which we live.

What exactly do we mean by "values?" The dictionary defines values as 1) the social principles, goals, or standards held or accepted by an individual, 2) that which is desirable or worthy of esteem. Your values determine how you and your family live. A modest list of values you hold might include honesty, importance of family, having fun, being physically fit, maintaining a certain income, and being well educated. There are numerous values that you hold that you may or may not be aware of. Your values may change from day to day, also. As your values change, your decisions and behavior change, too, and bring you new experiences.

New experiences themselves can cause you to change your values. Perhaps you get a ticket for driving too fast, so you decide to observe the speed limit from then on. Or perhaps someone close to you dies unexpectedly, and as a result you decide to let your loved ones know more frequently how much you love them.

Whether or not you're aware of it, you have priorities within your values. For example, you may value work more than you value time spent with your family. If this is the case, you may find that your children and your spouse are doing some negative things to get your attention. The atmosphere at home may feel debilitating or tense. However, if you change your priority to value your family more than you do work, you may find that your family becomes more supportive of you and your work. As a result, you feel nourished by your family.

One way you can determine what values you hold is to observe the quality of the life you live. If you don't feel nurtured within your family, look to see how much of yourself you're investing in them. What you spend time and money on can also reveal values.

To determine our values consciously requires honesty. For example, we might say we value the importance of living a healthful, unstressed life, but we continue to work at a very stressful job because we're afraid to quit and go without the level of income it provides. Perhaps we say it's important to us that our children don't watch too much television, but we allow them to watch a lot because we need a "baby sitter" while we do other things. Actions speak louder than words, so examine how you live to find out what you really value. If you don't like everything you see, you can change values and your behavior.

Eight ways to teach values

1. **Determine what values you want to live by.** Make a list of the top ten priorities for your family. This list will help you keep your attention on creating what you want your children to learn.

2. **Set rules around your values.** Let your values guide what rules your family will live by. For example, if family time is important to you at dinner, don't allow interruptions such as phone calls, or television. Require that everyone in the family be present, children and adults alike. If you value music, perhaps all the children ought to take some kind of music lessons (let each child choose what instrument to play so that she or he will be motivated).

3. **Be unrelenting about observing your values.** Sometimes in an attempt to make life easier for ourselves, we let things slide. This habit causes situations to become more frustrating, and time must be spent putting life in order again.

   If you don't find time to be with your family, it's likely that your family will cease to value being a family. Members may drift apart and it will be difficult to bring them back together. Start out in the manner you wish to go and stay with it.

4. **Reinforce your actions with your words.** Talk to chil-

dren about your actions. Tell them the good feeling that you get from following through on a value. For example, "I greeted people at church today. It really fills my heart with happiness when I can make people feel good."

5. **Look for teaching opportunities.** Be alert for stories from real life, television, books, and newspapers that illustrate a value you think is important. For example, my son loves football. My husband got him a book about a professional football player that is full of important values for my son. The author talks about the importance of holding on to a dream until it is realized, and also about perseverance, patience, humility, a balanced life with work and family, and a good education.

    Point out actions of neighbors and friends that demonstrate values. For example, I told my children about a friend who called me to apologize for lying to me the previous day. We discussed how much courage it took for her to call. I shared how much more I trusted her after her apology.

6. **Teach your child to prioritize.** Suppose your child values both friendships and good grades. When his friend calls him while he's studying, he'll have to choose which of these values is more important at that moment.

7. **If your child isn't honoring a value** you hold dear, you may want to ask yourself the following questions:

   • Am I sending a clear message? For example, you may really want the television off three days a week, but you only occasionally ask your family to turn it off. You have not been specific about what you want.

   • Are my actions congruent with my talk? A friend of mine was walking out of a store with his daughter when he noticed that the clerk had given him too much change. He headed back to the check-out counter as his daughter asked, "Why are you going back when she only gave you a dollar too much?" He replied, "My integrity is worth more than a dollar."

- Am I exerting too much control because I want my child to share my values? Sometimes children will get into power struggles over values if we're too pushy about them.
- If your teenager is rebelling against your values, it's not only normal but important for him to determine his own values. This is a stage, and he will grow out of it. He may not end up with all the same values you have, but most of them will probably be similar.

8. **Discuss your own struggles with your values.** Share with your child how you struggle with your own values. For example, "My boss wants me to do something that would save the company money. I don't want to do it because it will hurt the environment. I'm really struggling with this because I'm not sure what he'll do if I stick up for what I believe." Hearing you think about values helps your child clarify his own values. It also helps him feel less alone in his struggles.

Be insistent, subtle, creative, and inviting about teaching values. Don't give boring lectures, stern orders, or use "band wagon" approaches. Without values, our children are left to their own devices or pick up the values of their peers or the media. When you care enough to stick up for your values, your children develop a deep respect for you and themselves.

Adventures living with values

To raise the awareness of values within your family, try this game:

1. Choose a different value at the beginning of each week. Write it out and tape it to the refrigerator where everyone can see it daily.

2. Practice that value for a week by using it as a guide.

3. Get together at the end of the week in a pleasant place and share your stories of the adventures you each have had during the week of observing the value.

4. Decide if the value is one you wish to keep as a constant guide for behavior in your family. Discuss other ways to observe it.

5. Pick a new value for the next week, preferably one that is very different from last week's.

An example of how the game might work is this: a family picks responsible money management as the value. During the week, the parents develop a budget. One child makes a difficult decision about whether to buy a football or a skateboard. The teenager forgoes a shopping spree in favor of putting money into her savings account for school clothes later. The preschooler contributes his collection of pennies to buy guinea pig food. By the end of the week, the family will have other adventures revolving around money to share. Everyone in the family gets a chance to tell his or her story, and all listen respectfully. The value for the next week might be kindness to others.

4

Communication in Families

Children communicate their needs with words and actions. Loving, effective parents allow expression of needs, and show children how to express them in healthy ways.

Feelings

Many of us were not allowed to express a variety of intense emotions when we were growing up. Some parents said things like, "Want something to cry about? I'll give you something to cry about!" The expression of intense emotion scared people.

Vulnerability was equated with weakness. Even the dictionary gives a negative definition of the word: 1) capable of being wounded; open to attack 2) sensitive to criticism, temptations, influences, etc. Who would want to admit to vulnerability with a definition like that? We need a new definition that features vulnerability as openness: the ability to express honestly how one feels.

In this society, we criticize and try to stop or get rid of things that we don't understand. Parents tell children they are wrong to feel as they do. "You shouldn't hate your sister," or, "You should love Grandpa, even if he does say nasty things to you–he's your grandpa." Feelings are not right nor wrong. They just are. Much of children's misbehavior can be successfully redirected by simply allowing full expression (in a safe and appropriate manner) of their feelings.

Feeling stoppers

Feelings forced underground can cause misbehavior. Here is a list of "feeling stoppers," the actions parents take that cause children to stop expressing how they feel in order to protect themselves:

scolding	lecturing	name calling
solving problems	giving advice	punishing
moralizing	humiliating	pitying
making fun of	being sarcastic	rescuing
assuming	minimizing	interrupting
denying	imposing guilt	helping too much

We also squelch our children's feelings when we deny their expression by making these sorts of comments:

- "How can you be hungry? You just ate."

- "Your mom [dad] is only going to be gone for a few days, so there's no need to be sad."

- "Big boys [girls] don't cry."

- "This won't hurt."

- "That's not what you really want to do."

Comments like these deny your child the right to feel what he feels. They teach the child not to trust his judgment. What is he supposed to think, since he does feel what he feels? He is likely to be confused.

One reason we may repress our children's emotions is that we are uncomfortable with our own feelings. Parents who are in touch with their own feelings can respond in a more loving, accepting manner to their children when they express their feelings, including the "unpleasant" or intense ones.

Children try to protect themselves when parents use feeling stoppers. They think that it isn't safe to express who they really are, so they stuff their feelings—literally sometimes. One day, I watched a mother and her little boy, who was overweight, eating in a restaurant. The mother was incessantly nagging the boy. As she nagged, he stuffed food into his mouth as fast as he could. He seemed to be stuffing both food and feelings.

Recent findings also suggest that if you don't express your feelings, the feelings stay within and contribute to disease. The child who feels dominated by his parents and unable to express his feelings may take his frustrations out on his younger siblings, pets, or other property. If the situation becomes extreme enough, the result may be mental illness. An emotion repressed, persists. An emotion expressed, dissipates.

Feeling encouragers

These "feeling encouragers" show you ways to communicate that invite the expression of another person's feelings:

- Listen intently.

- Ask, "How does that make you feel?" or, "Tell me more."

- Affirm the feeling, "I can understand why you're angry."

- Be empathic, "If I were in your shoes, I would probably feel the same way."

- Explore with curiosity, "Is this the first time you've felt this way?"

- Ask questions to help your child solve the problem, "What would happen if . . . ?"

- To encourage her, say something about what she's expressing, "You're really clear about what you want to have different."

- When appropriate, share a similar experience of your own to help your child feel that he's not alone, "When I was your age, I had trouble asking girls out, too."

When a child expresses emotions, it's important that you first acknowledge, affirm, or empathize with her before you do any of the other suggestions to invite expression of feelings. The feeling of being understood and accepted is crucial in helping children work through their emotions. If you help your child find a solution before you help him to feel understood, he is more apt to get frustrated or defensive. He may stop expressing himself.

Effect of divorce on children

Those parents who have experienced divorce may have a difficult time acknowledging the effect it has on children. Children have a right to be angry when their parents divorce. Probably the one thing that a child wants most in his life is to have the two people he loves live together and love each other. Allow your child to express anger. Avoid feeling guilty or shameful about the divorce.

"Mom, I'm really angry you and Dad got a divorce!" said Chris. "Yes, I can understand that, Chris. What is it about the divorce that makes you the most angry?" asked Mom. Chris answered, "I don't like living in two houses. I don't know where my home is!" "It's confusing to you to have two homes," affirmed Mom. "Yeah," he said. "What else about the divorce

makes you angry?" she asked. "I don't like that we live so far apart," said Chris. [The families lived in different states.] "It would be great if we could jump in the car and see your dad!" said Mom. "Yeah!" exclaimed Chris. "Is there anything else you would like to ask me or tell me?" asked Mom. "Do you still love Daddy?" asked Chris. "Yes. There is a part of me that still loves your daddy very deeply. I respect your dad a lot but I don't want to be married to him," said Mom truthfully. Satisfied with her answer, her son smiled and kissed Mom goodnight.

Notice how Mom invited her son to talk freely about the divorce. She offered no guilt, shame, blame, or excuses in the conversation.

Frequently, all we need to do is just listen intently, hold the child, and be understanding. We get ourselves into a lot of trouble when we think we have to heal, fix, rescue, or convert.

Temper tantrums

Small children have temper tantrums for several reasons. They may have a basic need that isn't being met, or they have the goal of power, or they're testing limits, or they're simply frustrated. They communicate with the parent through a tantrum when they don't know any other way to do so, or when they don't want to communicate in another, more appropriate way.

One of the pitfalls in dealing with tantrums is that they conflict with our need to have things under control. We get angry with our children, and we want to quiet them as quickly as possible. What we need to do, instead, is take the time to figure out why our child is having a tantrum so that we can meet his needs.

Handling temper tantrums

Take care to handle your child gently during a tantrum, both physically and emotionally. Avoid punishing or threatening, arguing or debating, and dealing with the tantrum in public. Move to a more private place (a restroom, for example) if your child throws a tantrum out in public.

Take time to understand your child's signals so that you can take effective action. You can't negotiate with a child who is hungry, tired, ill, or hypersensitive. In those cases, get the child what she needs as quickly as possible. If you try negotiation with a child who is testing you, you may lose her respect. She may be testing you to see if you really mean what you say. However, negotiation works well with children who feel overpowered or frustrated.

This chart will help you figure out what your child is communicating and what your most effective action will be.

Child is:

Tired

What to do:

- Meet child's need.
- Minimize all talking that may lead to conflict.
- Hold or rock child.

Example:

- Take child to her bed or a quiet area to rest as soon as you can.

Hungry

What to do:

- Meet child's need.
- Minimize all talking that may lead to conflict.

Example:

- Give child something to eat as soon as possible, even if it's not a scheduled snack or meal time.

Ill

What to do:
- Meet child's need.
- Minimize all talking that may lead to conflict.
- Hold or rock child.

Example:
- Give child medical assistance if needed.

Hypersensitive

What to do:
- Remove object causing reaction as quickly as possible.
- Minimize all talking that may lead to conflict.

Example:
- If child's clothing is too tight, scratchy or hot, take it off as quickly as possible.

- If child is frustrated by abrupt changes, give advance warning or a choice. (Tommy, we'll be leaving in ten minutes," or, "Would you like to leave in 7 minutes or 10 minutes?")

Testing

What to do:
- Do not give in.
- Bring child to self-quieting place.
- Leave the room.
- Do the unexpected.

Example:

There are nonnegotiable boundaries that you have set, and your child testing you to see if you will hold the limits. You can discern this type of temper tantrum because you feel manipulated.

Powerless

What to do:

- Refuse to negotiate until child is calm and respectful.
- Acknowledge anger.
- Do win/win negotiation.
- Brainstorm solutions.
- Give child a sense of power.
- Fantasize with child about unfilled desire, if negotiation is impossible.

Example:

- "When you calm down, I am willing to discuss this with you," or, "Please use your negotiating voice."

- "I understand that you are angry."

- "I want you to win, and I would like to win, too. How could we work this out so we can both win?"

- Together write on a sheet of paper all possible solutions.

- Ask yourself, "How can I give my child more power in an appropriate way right now?

- "Yes, I would like ice cream, too. Two scoops with hot fudge, nuts, whipped cream, and a cherry on top. What would you have?"

Frustrated/Overwhelmed

What to do:

- Are your expectations too high?
- Break tasks down into manageable steps.
- Make sure child knows how to follow the directions.

Example:

- If your child is having a difficult time getting homework done, break it down into ten-minute segments of homework followed by five minutes of play. Repeat cycle until homework is finished. Set a timer for each segment to make process easy to follow.

Communication skills

A child has taken Mom's jewelry to play with and doesn't put it back. Mom might say to her child, "Why do you always take my things? I can never find them. If you don't stop taking my things, I'm going to lock my door!" Her threat is out of proportion to the misbehavior. Most likely, the child will get defensive or tune her out.

Mom could more effectively make her wishes about her jewelry known in the following manner:

"I feel frustrated when you take my jewelry because when I want it, it isn't where I left it. What I want is for you to put my jewelry back where you found it. What I love about you is your sense of style."

To communicate so that the other person is willing to listen, try this model:

"I feel [worried and angry]"

"When you [don't come home on time]"

"Because [I'm afraid you got hurt]"

"What I want is [for you to be on time, or call me if you'll be late]"

"What I love about you is [your joyous spirit and enjoyment of friends]"

If you try this method and it doesn't work, try using a logical consequence (see page 135).

When you communicate with your children, take responsibility for what you say and for what they hear. Watch facial expressions and body posture to make sure your child isn't discouraged by your communication. If your child starts explaining himself, defending himself, rolling his eyes, getting quiet, or looking disgusted, he's probably feeling defensive. If this happens, focus on creating closeness first. Do something encouraging to create a more open atmosphere. Then express your feelings and desire in the manner shown above.

Family meetings

Living in close proximity is challenging and requires cooperation among everyone in a family. I recommend that you have family meetings once a week. These meetings help children feel like they're involved in family decisions and, as a result, they feel more accountable to the family. Family meetings can create an incredible feeling of support and provide a forum for everyone to express their opinions in a safe place. To create that safety, it is essential that no criticism be allowed during these meetings.

It's also important that you set a day of the week and a specific time to have your meetings. I would suggest that you make that time a sacred one and that there be no exceptions or changes made to that time. If you keep making changes and exceptions, then your family members may stop respecting the meetings. Family meetings are effective forums in which to discuss matters such as these:

- Coordination of everyone's schedule for the week
- Meal plans and who will prepare them
- Vacation plans
- Household chores and who will do what
- Conflicts between family members
- Personal issues for which someone wants help
- Encouragement
- Budgeting
- Announcements
- Family entertainment
- Everyone's goals for the week and how the family can support them to accomplish their goals

If a conflict arises during the week, you can tell your children to bring it up at the family meeting. Stepping back from the conflict for a brief time gives everyone a chance to cool off. Postponement of a solution until the family meets as a group prevents the children from fighting for your attention.

Family meeting guidelines

Family meetings can be a very successful time in which you can solve problems, as well as have a lot of fun. Here are some ideas for the format of a family meeting.

Who and when. Hold the meeting once a week at a time when everyone in the family can attend. Make an agreement that whoever can't attend (for an acceptable reason) will still abide by decisions made at the meeting. If you find your children don't want to attend meetings, figure out why. Don't allow telephone interruptions or visitors.

Where. Sit at a table—a round one if you have it so that everyone is equal—rather than lounging on couches and easy chairs. Do not have a meal at the same time or do other tasks.

How. Elect a new leader and secretary at every meeting so that everyone gets a turn. The leader calls on people to speak; the secretary takes notes concerning what was discussed and decided. Later in the week, if there is disagreement about what was decided, the notes can be consulted.

- Begin the meeting with encouragement for each family member. Say, "What I love about you is . . . " and, "I'm grateful to you for . . . " and, "Thank you for . . . " Teach children to compliment others graciously and to receive compliments graciously by saying "thank you."

- Follow the agenda, which has been developed over the week as family members added items to it (a blackboard or paper on the refrigerator is a good place to post it). Let the person who has "the floor" hold an object to signify that he is speaking. A stuffed toy or some special object works. If you aren't holding the object, you are listening, not talking. Teach your children that if they have a complaint, they need to have a suggestion for a solution. Tell them, "A person who is not part of the solution is part of the problem."

• Make decisions by family consensus, not majority. That means everyone has to agree. Sometimes, it takes more than one family meeting to come to a decision. Aim for win/win decisions. Use the family meeting to practice this skill. Review the next week's calendar and plan family activities.

• Allow the leader to choose an enjoyable way to end the meeting. Some families like to have a snack or dessert, play a game or music together, or read a chapter in a book of interest to all. The goal is a pleasant activity which allows sharing. Make sure everyone feels good about the meeting, even when a decision gets postponed until the next meeting. Don't let anyone leave with unresolved issues.

How to handle difficult issues

If the meeting turns into a gripe session, stop it and do something to help the family feel close again. A great way to accomplish this is to have an encouragement feast. You want everyone to look forward to family meetings, and a gripe session is not the way to encourage repeat attendance.

During a family meeting, it's often necessary to address difficult issues or ask questions that may, at first, make children (and adults) feel defensive. It's essential that before doing this, you establish a trusting atmosphere. Once this friendly atmosphere is achieved, you can take a risk. Then, even if the child steps back in caution from your approach, you can still maintain the necessary emotional closeness. However, if you confront him when the relationship is disturbed, your child may feel like his position is vulnerable. If he backs off, you will have lost him.

"Joe, can I talk to you a minute?" asks Dad. "What?" Joe responds, in a gruff voice. [Caution: The relationship is disturbed—mend it before you continue.] "Sounds like you're expecting another lecture. Guess I do lecture you a lot, don't I?" says Dad, thoughtfully. "Ah, you aren't so bad."

responds Joe. "Well, sometimes I catch myself treating you like you don't know anything and that's not how I feel," admits Dad. "Don't worry about it, Dad. What did you want, anyway?" [Dad has now improved the relationship by talking about some of his own imperfections; it's now safe to confront Joe.] "Well, I wanted to see if we could work out a better way of keeping the family room clean. Do you have any ideas?" [If Dad had started directly with this last question, Joe would have resisted finding a solution.]

With practice, you will find that you can interpret your child's response. You will find this a valuable tool when you are discussing and resolving relationship difficulties in the family meeting.

Steps for conflict resolution

As often as possible, solve problems in a win/win style. Your child will feel good and be more cooperative; so will you. The brainstorming process that is part of negotiation may seem tedious and cumbersome at first. With practice, you will find that it comes more easily, with efficient and rewarding results. Here is an example of how it works:

Problem: Three-year-old Joey comes into Mom's bed during the night. Mom is angry that he disturbs her sleep.

Step 1. Ask permission to work on the problem with the other person. "Joey, I want some time to brainstorm with you. Is this a good time?"

Step 2. Write down on paper what result you want from the conversation. Also, write why you want it, clearly, simply, without guilt, blame, shame, or exaggeration. Use "I" statements (see page 67). "It disturbs my sleep when you come into my bed during the night. I want you to sleep in your own bed."

Step 3. Ask your child to share how he feels, and tell you what he wants (gather information). You need to know so that you can arrive at a solution that allows both of you to win. "I get lonely in my bed all by myself. I want to sleep with some-one," says Joey.

Step 4. Make a list of the possible solutions to the problem on your paper. Be creative, and don't judge a solution at this point. Sometimes it helps the process to put down things you think are crazy, just to loosen up. The important rule of brainstorming is that you don't criticize or reject any idea at this listing stage. Anything goes! If your brainstorming part-ner is critical and won't become positive, stop the process and wait until later to try again.

Step 5. When you've thought up all the ideas you can, give the list to your child first. Have him cross out any idea he doesn't like; then you take the list and cross out the ideas you don't like. You read the list to children who can't read by themselves and help them cross off ideas.

Step 6. Pick one idea or a combination of ideas from those remaining on the list to be the solution to the problem. In the spirit of win/win, make sure you are both satisfied. Read your child's body language and tone of voice to make sure he really is happy with the solution. If he says "okay," but doesn't mean it, the solution won't work. In that case, choose a dif-ferent solution.

Step 7. Use the solution for a specified time period. If that solu-tion doesn't work, brainstorm again for a new one. Don't give up, and do keep a positive attitude.

Here is the list Mom and Joey made:

- Mom could let Joey sleep in her bed.

- Joey could stay in his bed.

- Joey could sleep in Mom's bed twice a week.

- Mom could sleep in Joey's bed in his room.

- Joey could sleep in his sleeping bag on the floor next to Mom's bed.

- Joey could sleep with his stuffed animal.

- Joey could sleep with his cat.

- Mom could have another baby who could sleep in Joey's room.

Mom and Joey decided that Joey could sleep in a sleeping bag on the floor in Mom's room two nights a week. Both Mom and Joey were happy with this solution.

The win/win nature of conflict resolution suits problem solving with teenagers as well.

Problem: Mom and fifteen-year-old Tamara, Joey's sister, agreed to work on a problem Mom had. Tamara was often late getting home in the evening. Mom didn't want to worry about her.

The two of them came up with these ideas in their brainstorming session:

- Tamara could go without a curfew.

- Mom could tell her that if she wasn't home by 11 p.m., she had to come home at 10 p.m. the next night she was out.

- Mom could lock the doors so Tamara couldn't get into the house.

- Tamara could wake Mom up when she gets home, so Mom won't worry.

- Mom could set an alarm and, if Tamara isn't home when it goes off, Mom will call the police.

Mom and Tamara decided that Mom would set an alarm for 11:15 p.m. If Tamara got home by 11 p.m., she would turn it off. If the alarm went off, then Mom would start looking for Tamara.

5

Which Way to Responsibility?

Children who learn to be responsible for their actions and their own well-being have a great advantage in life. In order for children to be responsible, however, they need to know how to think creatively and to solve problems. As a parent, you will only be comfortable giving responsibility to your child if you believe he stands a good chance of handling it.

Parents who ask children questions, instead of providing answers, help them learn to think through problems and look at different possibilities for action. Once a child is able to think about problems, she can take the next step: making decisions.

Teach your child to make decisions

One of the most needed skills in an adult is the ability to make decisions. This skill is based on considering alternatives. In the short run, it's easier for parents to make decisions for their children. What is appropriate decision making on behalf of a two-year-old becomes appropriate decision making by a five-year-old, and so on as the child grows, however. Recall that you are working yourself out of the job of parenting gradually.

A toddler was screaming because she was put in her crib for the night. Her dad came to the door and said, "If you want to continue screaming, I will close the door. If you decide to be quiet, I will leave it open." The little girl thought for a moment and then sat down and began to look at a book quietly. Her dad left the door open and went back to his activity.

A woman's seven-year-old nephew asked, "Do you think it would be all right if I brought these candies with me to the funeral?" His aunt replied, "Think about the situation. We are going to the funeral home which is a very quiet place to say good-bye and be respectful. When you decide what you want to do, let me know." The boy pondered his dilemma for a few moments and then told his aunt that he had decided not to bring the candies with him.

A teenager asked his mom at 9 p.m. if he could go to his friend's house. Her first urge was to say, "No, you haven't done your homework, and it's late." Instead she "bit her tongue" and said, "Think about how much time you need to do your homework and how much time you need for sleep, then decide." Her son decided to go to his friend's house for 15 minutes. Mom knew that if she had told her son what to do, he would have rebelled and gone off for half the night. Given the opportunity, he made a responsible decision.

In each situation above, the adults expected the children to think and make reasonable decisions. The teenager appropriately had a more complex situation to think about than the boy or the toddler. It would have been easy for the adults to tell the children what to do. Instead, each child was given time to think and allowed to make his or her decision.

Trust your child

One thing I appreciated about my parents was that when I became a teenager, they didn't tell me what time to be home, but would ask me, "What time will you be home?" They trusted me and respected my ability to make a responsible decision. As a result, I made a conscious effort to live up to that trust. I came home on time because we shared mutual respect, not because I was afraid of what they might do or say to me.

Teach your child to trust his intuition

One way you can help your child make decisions is by helping him trust his intuition about what is right. When your child asks you what to do, instead of telling him, ask him to calm his mind and get his answer from inside himself. If the answer he gets is based on fear, tell him to look again for a different answer. Encourage your child to think in this manner:

Alicia approached her mother, crying, "Blaire doesn't want to play with me anymore." After some discussion about how Alicia feels, Mom asks, "What will you do?" Alicia says, "I don't know." Mom suggests, "Why don't you get real quiet and ask yourself what the best thing to do would be."

Several minutes later Alicia returns to tell Mom that she has decided that she isn't going to play with Blaire anymore. Mom observes that this decision is probably based on fear and suggests that Alicia try the quiet method again. This time Blaire returns happier, yet more determined. "I decided to call up Blaire to see if she's still mad at me," she reports. Mom encourages, "That's brave of you."

Tell your child the truth

The reality of what you say must correspond to the child's intuitive sense of what is true and real. To act on their intuition, children need to believe that their perceptions are accurate.

One day my son asked, "Mommy, why are you mad?" Caught off guard, I said, "I'm not mad." Then I realized I had been reviewing mentally a conflict with someone from earlier in the day. My son's intuition was correct. "You're right, I was angry about something that happened at work. Thanks for helping me recognize that," I told him.

Children are very sensitive to the "vibes" around them. When we lie or deny an emotion, we teach them to doubt their intuition. Sometimes we lie to protect children. Or so we think. They usually know when something is wrong, and their imaginations can create a situation worse than the real one. At the very least, we cause great confusion. Confusion gets in the way of good decision making.

Teach your child to get what she wants

It's your child's job to learn how to make herself happy. When we entertain our children, take care of all their needs, smooth over the troubles in their lives at every turn, and provide material goods for their comfort and pleasure, we allow them to develop an attitude that others should make life exciting and comfortable for them. A statement like, "I'm bored," means, "I shouldn't have to be responsible for making my life the way I want it to be. Someone else should do it for me." The child who is entertained tends to be attracted as an adolescent to drugs or excessive television, neither of which require much investment of her own energy. She has not learned to think about that which makes her genuinely happy.

When your child says, "I'm bored," avoid the temptation to say, "Well, you could call up Susie or you could finger paint." Instead, say in a friendly tone of voice, "What will you do?" If she asks for suggestions in an appropriate tone of voice (without whining, pouting, or looking sad), then you may want to give an occasional suggestion, but avoid making the arrangements. Let her take responsibility for them. If your child's tone is inappropriate, you may want to leave the room or ignore the request until she asks in a pleasant tone.

Love

Teach your children how to take responsibility for the love they want. We can't expect other people to read our minds and know when we need outward expressions of love and affection.

One way for your children to develop this skill is to have family "love bags." Each family member has a separate bag. In each bag, the child puts small strips of paper on which he has written something that would help him feel loved. For example, "Read me a book, please," "Rub my feet, please," "Tell me something you love about me, please," "Listen to me for fifteen minutes, please," and so forth. Make sure the request can be fulfilled at the time it's made and requires nothing more than time and attention. Requests to buy things are not suitable for the love bag. You don't want your child to associate being loved with money or things. When your child feels discouraged or unloved, he can take his love bag to a willing family member to draw from it and fulfill his request.

This is also a great way to circumvent discipline problems. Instead of misbehaving to get your attention, your child can bring you his love bag and get love in an appropriate way.

Love bags work for every family member. You and your spouse may want to have a separate, private love bag for yourselves! It's never too late to take responsibility for your own happiness.

Teach your child to give 100%

Many of us have learned to get by in life with little investment of ourselves. Encourage your child to put her all into the things she does. Help her recognize the feeling of pride that comes from giving 100% of attention and effort. Teach your child to set her own goals and do her best to achieve them.

Emphasize "personal best," rather than a comparison to someone else's achievement. Ask, "Did you do your best?" instead of, "Were you the best?" When you do not compare your child to someone else, she is more likely to enjoy doing her best. If she knows how to recognize her own effort, she won't be so discouraged when someone else is better than she is. There will always be someone better, so it's good to learn early in life that comparisons generally lead to a feeling of defeat.

Some children are able to look at another child's or older person's accomplishment and see areas and ways to improve their own. This is legitimate observation provided it doesn't lead to the child giving up.

Go the "extra mile"

We're so thankful when our children actually finish the tasks we asked them to do that we forget to teach them the value of going the extra mile. You know what a great feeling it is when you put forth that extra effort, even if no one else notices. Teach your children by acknowledging their efforts, starting when they are babies and toddlers. In time, they will internalize your encouragement. They will feel pride when they put flowers on the table or fold the napkins a special way, check their homework, or sweep the walk when only asked to sweep out the garage.

Encourage altruistic behavior

Allow your child opportunities to give without expecting something in return. Children like to feel good about themselves, and helping others can provide these good feelings. A "thank you" may be appropriate, but an offer of money can completely spoil the experience for the child. If you wish to encourage altruism, make sure you don't confuse your child with material reward.

Expect your child to be capable

We often do things for our children because we can do them more quickly and efficiently. We are, however, robbing children of the chance to learn by experience and to build self-confidence. When you act as if your child can handle a situation, she senses that you have confidence in her. She will feel encouraged to do things beyond what she thinks are currently possible.

Be particularly wary about doing something for a child who says, "I can't" when you've already seen that he can. Let him practice and gain more confidence in his abilities.

Nate is trying to buckle his shoes. "Mommy, I can't!" he wails. Mother, who is not in a hurry, says in a friendly voice, "I think you can handle it." She smiles at Nate and leaves the room.

Mother's tone of voice was very accepting. She wasn't annoyed with Nate. She was telling him that she had confidence in him, both with her words and her actions. If you leave the room, you will find it easier to keep from coaxing or becoming annoyed at your child's efforts to get you to do the task for him. Give your child the benefit of the doubt. You may be surprised!

Ask for your child's help

Children sometimes feel like midgets in a world of competent giants. They overestimate how much parents can do (some younger children feel as though parents are perfect) and underestimate their own worth. A very effective way to build a child's self-confidence is to ask for his help. When a friend has asked you for help, do you remember how important and worthwhile you felt? Give your children the chance to feel that way, too. My young son's fresh view-point really helped me one day:

I came home upset about a conflict I'd had with one of my employees. Five-year-old Tyler could see that I was unhappy and asked me what was wrong. I told him about the situation and asked him if he had any suggestions about what I should do. He thought for a moment. Valentine's Day had just passed, and he suggested that I give my co-worker one of his Valentine cards. At first, I criticized the idea in my head, thinking how silly it would be to do that. Then I thought, "Why not!"

Tyler and I searched through the garbage and found a Valentine that didn't have too many coffee grounds smeared on it. I slipped it into an envelope and the next day I gave it to my employee, saying, "I felt so bad about what happened between us yesterday. Tyler suggested that I give you this Valentine." She started to cry, I started to cry, and we resolved the conflict right then and there. That night, I shared with Tyler what had happened and thanked him for helping me solve my problem. Imagine how proud of himself he felt for being able to help his grown-up mom solve one of her work problems!

Older children can really surprise you. Shortly before the camp I ran was to begin, I received a call from a father who had enrolled his two sons. He told me that he had suffered a major financial crisis in his business and he was unable to send his boys to camp. He wanted some suggestions on how he could break the bad news to his boys. I suggested that rather than telling the boys he couldn't afford to send them to camp, he ask for their help in deciding how to handle the crisis. Several evenings later he phoned and told me:

I said to my sons, "Boys, I've made a mistake in my business and lost a big order. Because of this, we're going to be very short of money for a while. Do you guys have any ideas that might help me solve this problem?" The boys' response was amazing. They volunteered to give up camp. They also offered to start turning off unnecessary lights and to get paper routes. But the greatest benefit is that their eagerness to help has made the whole problem less of a threat to me. I feel like I have the support of my family. I made a huge mistake, yet the family is closer than ever!

This father's willingness to talk about his mistakes and to ask for the children's help avoided a possible family crisis and made him feel accepted even though he was at fault. He gave his children the opportunity to help, to feel like their ideas made a difference and, perhaps most importantly, showed them that admitting a mistake is a responsible thing to do.

Remind your child that she makes a difference

Children, especially teenagers, feel like they are "just children" and can't really make much of a difference in the world. They tend to feel that the adults have all the authority and what they think, feel, and do doesn't really matter. Remind your children frequently that they do make a difference. Tell them when their suggestions or efforts help you or someone else. For example, "You know, that advice you gave me about your little sister was very helpful. I tried what you suggested, about not giving in to her, and it really worked."

Give your child responsibilities

Sometimes parents only give children responsibilities that relate to their own personal effects, such as picking up their belongings. One of the best ways you can teach your child helpfulness is to provide many opportunities for him to contribute to the family. Avoid giving him only the "low dignity jobs," such as taking out the garbage and cleaning up the dog's messes. Include tasks that get more recognition, such as preparing the family budget, shopping, or cooking a meal. Let him know how important his contribution is.

Children learn responsibility by being responsible for tasks appropriate to their age. I could stand and watch an expert hit tennis balls forever, but unless I'm given the opportunity to experience the results of my mistakes and the joy of my successes with that ball and racket, it's unlikely that I'll develop my tennis skills by simply observing. Likewise, a child will never learn to get herself out of bed on time if her parent takes the responsibility away from her by waking her every day. She needs to feel the consequences of over-sleeping and the pride of self-reliance when she gets up on time.

Be sure to give responsibility in an empowering way. For example, instead of saying, "It's about time you started doing your own laundry," say, "I've noticed that you are handling responsibility for picking up after yourself really well. I think you're ready to learn how to do your own laundry."

On the next page is a list of age-appropriate tasks. Teach skills needed and supervise carefully as long as needed for safety. The list is by no means complete, but serves as a guide for parents who don't realize how much their children can contribute from an early age.

Hand down responsibility

Each month, ask yourself, "What am I doing for my child this month that he may be ready to take responsibility for doing on his own?" Maybe a preschooler is now capable of making his own bed in the morning, or an older child is now ready to do her own laundry, or a teenager can make his own dental appointments. Make sure you turn over responsibilities you know they can handle. A child can only take full responsibility for something he or she has the skills to do.

These gradual gifts of responsibility will prove to be far less overwhelming to your child than if you wait until he is sixteen, eighteen, or twenty-one and suddenly declare, "You're an adult now–handle things on your own." If you implement this plan, you'll be amazed to see how much responsibility a child can learn to manage and enjoy at even a young age.

Tasks Children Can Do to Learn Responsibility

18 months old– 3 years old

Turn off lights while being carried

Carry in the newspaper or mail

Get own cereal or snack from kid-friendly containers

Wash tables and counters with damp sponge

Pick up toys and clothes

Put soiled or wet diaper in the diaper pail

Wash vegetables, tear lettuce, stir

Help set the table

Feed and water pets

Help clean up after meals and play

Wake up sibling

Run simple errands around the house

Help put groceries away

Carry in light groceries

Scramble eggs, make toast

Help make beds

Put plastic dishes in the dishwasher

Make salads

Bring recyclables to the garage

Lead family prayers

Put own clothes away

Take clothes out of the dryer

Tell you when the traffic light turns green

Clear dishes from the table

Seal and stamp envelopes

4–6 years old

All of the above, plus more:

Help find grocery items in the store

Help fold towels and wash cloths

Pour things

Give you a back rub or foot rub

Help measure ingredients

Count goods at the grocery store

Water plants

Sort white clothes from dark clothes for laundry

Help with vacuuming, sweeping, and dusting

Take library books and videos to or from the car

Put gas in the car

Help younger siblings

Help plant a garden

Wash the floor

Put dishes in dishwasher

Measure soap for dishwasher and start cycle

Be responsible for compost buckets

Haul things in the wagon
Assist in meal planning
Make a simple meal
Empty dishwasher and stack dishes on counter
Rake leaves for short periods of time
Help wash pets
Prepare own lunch
Walk well-behaved pets
Carry in firewood
Start to manage his own money

7–10 years old

All of the above, plus more:
Get herself up in the morning
Help wash and vacuum car
Wash dishes
Fix snacks and light meals
Help read recipes
Run washing machine and dryer
Change sheets on the bed
Help with projects around house
Address and stuff envelopes
Read to younger siblings
Bathe younger siblings

11–15 years old

All of the above, plus more:
Baby sit
Cook meals

Buy groceries from a list
Wash windows
Change light bulbs
Make appointments
Order out for family
Wax car
Mow lawn
Operate saws for home projects
Help in parent's business

16–18 years old

All of the above, plus more:
Run errands
Balance family check book
Handle their own checking account
Maintain car
Help with family budgets
Take care of house/garden/yard
Take care of animals
Help younger children with homework
Take care of siblings

6

Why Do Children Misbehave?

Children usually misbehave because they are fulfilling a need. Your child is communicating with you about his needs when he misbehaves. In order to teach your child a better way to tell you what he needs, you must figure out what goal he has in mind. Identify your child's goal before you decide how to discipline him. This is easier to do than you may think.

A single mother, her boyfriend, and her seven-year-old son Mark were driving along in the car. Mark kept interrupting the grown-ups' conversation. Mom asked, "Honey, this behavior isn't like you. Is there something you need?" Mark answered, "Yeah, when you're with him, I feel invisible." Mom thought for a moment and realized she and her friend really weren't paying much attention to Mark. When they began to include Mark in their conversation, he stopped bugging his mother. His need for attention was being met.

It is important to understand why your child behaves as he does, so that your response is the right one. For example, if you view a toddler who tries to flush a roll of toilet paper down the toilet as "bad," you have failed to recognize the toddler's need to become competent. He learns how the toilet works by exploring, and until he tries to flush the roll of toilet paper and sees the result, he will not understand why he can't flush something so large. If, on the other hand, you view his experiment for what it is, you can show him what he can flush safely.

The same is true for children whose goals are to meet other needs. Your job as a parent is to meet their needs appropriately. In the process, they will be learning how to meet their own needs as they grow.

Importance of the correct diagnosis

Three people visited the doctor for three different reasons.

Doctor: "What seems to be your problem?"
Patient 1: "I have a headache."
Patient 2: "My foot hurts a lot."
Patient 3: "My arm hurts whenever it's cold outside."
Doctor: "I can help you all! Since none of you feel good, I'll take out your gall bladders. Why, just six months ago I had a patient who didn't feel good. I took out his gall bladder, and now he feels fine!"

Would you trust a doctor who thinks like this? Of course not: a) he didn't take the time to make a proper diagnosis, b) he assumed everyone's problem was the same, c) he believed one solution would work for every problem. The necessity for correct diagnosis is obvious in the medical field. We sometimes overlook its importance in parenting.

Unfortunately, no one discipline method will be effective in every situation. To determine what method to use, you have to take time to think about why your child is behaving in a certain way. Until you understand the goal of your child's misbehavior, you can't be sure which action will be most effective.

Goal of attention

The manner in which parents respond to their children is very important. Children often base future behavior on their parents' reactions to what they do. Here is a perceptive child who gets attention for negative behavior because she couldn't succeed in getting it any other way.

Twenty-month-old Mariana sat quietly rocking in her rocking chair as her father read his newspaper. She began to rock faster and faster until the chair tipped over, spilling her to the floor with the chair on top of her. Immediately, her father dropped his newspaper, ran over, picked up the chair, and rescued his daughter. He carried her in his arms to his chair and spent fifteen minutes comforting her on his lap.

About three days later, Mariana approached her father who again was reading the paper. She tried climbing onto his lap, but Dad was being uncooperative. He gently brushed her aside, saying, "Not now, Honey. I want to read the paper." The little girl walked over to the rocking chair, looked back at her father who was absorbed in the daily news, and tipped the chair forward until its back rested on the floor. Quietly, she squirmed under the chair and started crying. Success! Dad threw down his newspaper, rushed to pick her up, and consoled her in his lap again.

Children need and are entitled to our attention if they are to grow to healthy adulthood. They know this instinctively and often interpret negative attention as better than no attention at all.

Mother and her best friend are visiting over coffee. Four-year-old Billy runs into the room and stands behind the sofa. In a whiny voice, he asks, "Mom, where's my airplane?" Mom stops talking to her friend and says, "I'm busy now. It's in your room." She resumes talking to her friend. Billy interrupts again, "Where in my room?" This time Mom interrupts her friend and says, "In your toy chest. . . . I'm sorry, what were you saying?" Mom turns her attention back to her friend. Billy persists, "Would you help me find it?" Mother jumps from the sofa in exasperation, "Oh, all right! But when I find it, I want you to play with it in your room so I can visit with my friend."

Billy's request for help sounds innocent enough, right? However, the clue that it isn't lies in Mother's feeling of exasperation. What would be a more acceptable way for Billy to behave while his mother visits with her friend? He could respect her statement that she's busy and leave her alone. He could find the toy himself, or play with something else. What does he really want from his mother? He wants to be the center of her attention; he may be wondering if she loves him if he isn't.

In this example, Billy's inappropriate demands for attention were made in a relatively positive way. When a child is more discouraged, his demands for attention may be more negative. For example, the child might start playing with something he's not allowed to play with or pick a fight with his brother or sister. Some other ways of getting attention are whining, dawdling, forgetting, acting helpless, interrupting, or repeating an annoying behavior.

Remember that it is okay for a child to want attention; it's a legitimate human need and is shared by all children and adults. What you are dealing with is the child's inappropriate ways of trying to get legitimate attention.

The way you can identify the misbehaving child's goal is by the way you feel and by how you would usually respond to his behavior. For the child whose goal is attention, you will feel frustrated and annoyed. You tend to respond by giving negative attention. Not all children use negative behavior to get attention, however. Consider the child who is being (too) good in order to get attention. It is important for her to be good and to please you. This child is often called "goodie-goodie" at home and "teacher's pet" at school. Again, your response to her behavior is the important clue. When you feel annoyed by this child's striving to please you or be good, it is an indication that her goal is attention.

Redirecting the goal of attention

There are four steps to redirecting misbehavior when the goal is attention:

1. **Make no eye contact with the child who is misbehaving.**

2. **Do not talk to the child.**

   The first two steps describe how to ignore the child when she is trying to get your attention inappropriately. Ignoring is not enough, however. If you only ignore, your child's behavior is likely to get worse. Be sure to go on to step 3.

3. **Do something physical to make the child feel loved.** The best way to do this is to rub her back or stroke her hair. Don't pat your child's head because this is demeaning; she'll feel like a baby.

4. **Take action immediately.** Do the first three steps—no eye contact, no words, and some physical action to make the child feel loved—as soon as you start feeling annoyed. Do not wait. If you wait, you'll start to get angry. It would then be difficult not to react angrily. When you're angry, it's hard to do something to make the child feel loved.

When you practice doing all four steps correctly, your child has to rethink her behavior. She's used to thinking, "As long as I keep an adult busy with me, then I'm loved." Now she sees that she's loved without the adult having to "keep busy" with her.

As a father talked across the fence in his backyard to his neighbor, his daughter Teresa kept interrupting him. His goal was for her to wait patiently until he finished. He wanted her to say politely, "Excuse me," as he had pre-

viously taught her to do. However, Teresa had other plans. She began whining immediately, "Daaaddy!" Dad kept on talking with his neighbor, did not talk to Teresa or make eye contact with her. He lovingly started rubbing her back as she stood whining beside him. She continued to whine for a few seconds and then stopped. She patiently waited for a break in their conversation and said, "Excuse me, Daddy," very politely.

In order for successful redirection to occur, it's vital that you take time to be with your child when she's not competing for attention. This helps to reinforce the appropriate behavior you desire.

Teach your child how to get your attention in appropriate ways. One mother taught her daughter to say, "I need some attention, Mommy," instead of acting out to get it. When her daughter said those words, Mom would either give her the attention right then or she would negotiate a specific, agreed upon time to be with her child in a genuinely attentive way.

A busy parent can make "dates" with her children. Each child gets a separate date during the week. The dates may consist of a breakfast, lunch with the child at school, roller skating, fishing, etc. These one-on-one times are essential. It's much easier for a child to share intimate thoughts and feelings when he's alone with you, in a relaxed atmosphere. If he feels he has a close relationship with you, he becomes more respectful and more cooperative. When children can get our attention in appropriate ways, they are less likely to try to get it in inappropriate ways.

Fathers often play "rough and tumble" with both their little sons and daughters. When their daughters start physically developing in the teen years, fathers usually quit tumbling with them. It is important for fathers to replace the playtime and attention of the childhood years with some other activity so that their daughters don't feel abandoned. For example, one father started taking tennis lessons with his daughter. Another father started a nightly routine of reading a chapter in a novel they had picked out together.

You might be thinking that the steps for redirecting attention won't work for your child and you may be right, especially if your child has a different goal than attention. So read on!

The goal of power

"Turn the TV off," Dad said to Jordan. "It's time for bed." "Aw, Dad, let me finish watching this one show. It'll be over in thirty minutes," challenges Jordan. "No, I said turn it off!" Dad demands with a stern look on his face. "Why? I'll just watch fifteen minutes, okay? C'mon, let me watch it. You never let me stay up late anymore," Jordan protests. Dad's face is getting red and he points his finger at Jordan, "Did you hear what I said, young man? I said off with the TV . . . NOW!"

Father feels angry at being challenged. His natural inclination is to use more force. To help you tell the difference between the goals of power and attention, watch what your child does. When you punish your child who is seeking attention, his misbehavior stops because he has achieved his goal. He has your attention. However, when you punish a child who has the goal of power, his misbehavior usually escalates rather than stops. Even if the behavior stops temporarily, he will have a defiant look as if he were saying, "You can stop me now, but I'll defeat you later!'

When you find yourself in power struggles with your children, change the question from, "What can I do to control this situation?' to "How can I give my child more power in this situation?" In exchange for power, your child will give you cooperation.

When Tyler was three years old, he and I went grocery shopping around 5:30 p.m. Big mistake! I was tired and he was tired. I was in a hurry to get home to prepare supper, so I put him in the shopping cart to expedite the shopping. As I hurried down each aisle grabbing what I needed, Tyler began throwing the groceries out of the cart. At first, I said calmly, "Tyler, please stop." He ignored me and continued throwing things out of the cart. Then I said more harshly, "Tyler, STOP IT!" As my voice rose in anger, his behavior escalated. Next, he took my purse and dumped the contents all over the floor. I grabbed his small arms. I wanted to shake him!

At that instant, I understood how child abuse occurs. I took a few steps back and counted to ten, which is a method I use to calm myself. As I was counting, I realized that Tyler had no power in that situation. He had been

*forced into a cold, hard shopping-cart seat as his harried mother rushed through
the store picking up items he didn't even care about. I asked myself, "What
can I do to make Tyler feel more powerful in this situation?"*

*I decided one thing I could do instantly would be to ask Tyler's advice
about shopping. "Do you think Snoopy [our dog] would like this kind of
dog food or that kind?" "What vegetables do you think Dad would like?" By
the time we moved into the next aisle, I was amazed at how cooperative Tyler
had become. I thought someone had swapped children with me, but I knew
it was me that had changed, not my son.*

Parents think of incredibly creative ways to give their children
power when they put their minds to it. I have more examples than
I can possibly relate in this book. One of my favorites is this
mother's story:

*Three-year-old Katy would not put on her seat belt and keep it on. Her
mother would get to work late, feeling tired and frustrated even though the day
had hardly begun. No matter how much she argued and threatened, Katy
would not cooperate. So Mom changed her approach. She decided to make
Katy the Captain of the Seat Belts. Mom could not start the car until Katy
told her that everyone in the car had their seatbelts on. Katy felt important
and powerful because she was now in charge of whether or not they could
depart. Her behavior changed from defiant to cooperative overnight.*

Redirecting the goal of power

There are several surefire ways to give children appropriate power
that will get you out of power struggles. There are also techniques
that you can use to prevent the power struggle from occurring in
the first place. Different situations call for different actions.

Offer your child choices

You can easily decrease the number of power struggles in your
household by giving your child choices as often as is possible and
reasonable. A choice is different from a command. Compare "Stop
that!" with "Would you like to play with your truck here without
bumping the walls, or would you like to play with it in your sand-

box?" Children who are given choices learn to make decisions on their own, are less dependent on their parents and other adults, and are less rebellious. They also learn to recognize the connection between their decisions and what happens to them.

When you offer a choice, keep these cautions in mind:

- Be sure the choices you give are both acceptable to you.

- If the child doesn't choose either option, offer another choice that allows you to take action. For example, "Would you like to walk or would you like me to carry you?"

- If your child does not choose, assume she doesn't want the freedom to choose. Choose for her and act. In the example above, pick her up gently and carry her from the room.

Some other examples of simple choices are these:
- "Would you like to dress in the house or in the car?"
- "Would you prefer to brush your teeth now or after we read ?
- "Would you like to feed the dog or take out the garbage?"
- "Would you like to baby-sit Leon while I run to the store or would you like to go to the store for me?"

- Be sure that neither of the choices you offer is a punishment, for then there is no choice. For example, "Would you like to play outside or go to your room without dinner?" offers no real choice.

Sometimes it's hard to think of choices to offer children. This may be because you don't feel like you have many choices in your own life. Practice giving yourself choices. If you don't want to wash the dishes, what other choices are there? Ask your husband or the children to do them; use throwaway dishes instead; leave the dishes until the next day; or hire someone else to do them may be among the possibilities you think of.

Many doctors who have learned about redirecting children's behavior instead of issuing commands have eased the tensions of office visits considerably. When a child needs a shot, she is given a choice of which arm to get it in or of which nurse to give it. She can have a choice of colorful Band-Aids. She can decide whether to sit or lie down or stand up when the shot is given. Even though she may not be happy about the shot, the choices give her some control and responsibility in a situation that may feel out of control.

Increase your child's sense of self-worth

Everyone needs to feel valuable and worthy. The more opportunities you give your child to feel valuable, the less likely she is to misbehave.

It takes a bit of thought to provide opportunities that genuinely increase a child's sense of self-worth. You usually have to change how you do something as well. Thoughtful parents attest to the positive results of their efforts. Here are three examples, representing experiences with a preschooler, an elementary school child, and a teenager. Notice the effort the parents put into finding ways for their children to feel valuable, which resulted in an improved self-opinion for the children.

Mother let three-year-old Angie determine what color to paint the living room! Mother picked two paint samples, both of which she liked. Then she asked her daughter, "Angie, I'm debating about the color to paint the living room. Would you pick which color you think it should be?" Mom said that when her friends came over, she would make sure Angie overheard her say that Angie had picked the color of the living room. Mom said that she could see how proud Angie was of herself for having made that decision.

Twelve-year-old Damion did poorly at school and homework was a struggle. Dad decided to do something to make his son feel valuable. He taught his son how to do the payroll for his three employees at his floral shop. By the end of the year, Damion was doing the payroll so skillfully that he began doing it for two other florists in town. Not surprisingly, his grades also improved.

Dad had guessed that one reason his son was getting bad grades was to get even for the lack of quality time they had shared. Since Dad wasn't home much, the time he and his son spent together on the family business improved their relationship. By allowing and teaching Damion to help him, Dad started to value his son and acknowledge him for his help.

↻

Stepmother Monique was having difficulty establishing a relationship with her fourteen-year-old stepdaughter Anna. She decided to ask Anna to assist her in choosing some new clothes for her husband. She shared with Anna her lack of knowledge about current fashions and asked for her advice. Anna agreed to help out, and together they shopped for clothes for Anna's father. The shopping trip provided attractive clothes for Dad, but more importantly it helped Anna feel valuable and was the turning point in the relationship between stepmother and stepdaughter.

Negotiate win/win solutions

Most of us were not taught the concept of win/win negotiation as children. Our experience involves win/lose or lose/lose situations. The most effective negotiations are those when both parties strive for a solution in which both win and are happy with the end result. To arrive at such a solution, each person must listen intently to what the other person wants, while staying committed to his or her wish or need.

The essence of negotiation is that each party thinks of ideas that will allow both parties to get what they want. Neither tries to talk the other out of or into anything different from what each wants. Both parties keep thinking of solutions until each has exactly what he or she wants. Sometimes each person is delightfully surprised because the results are better than either expected. The concept of win/win takes time to implement at first, but the rewards are well worth that extra time and patience. The process becomes easier as the whole family develops this skill. It takes practice, like all the other good parenting techniques.

I was going to do a lecture in my hometown and I asked my son, who was eight at the time, to support me by going along. As I was headed out the door for the lecture, I glanced down at Tyler's jeans. There, poking out of a large hole, was his knee. My heart sank. I promptly asked him to change. He said, *"No,"* and *I found myself engaged in a power struggle with him.*

As soon as I realized what we were doing, I stopped. After a moment's thought, I decided to use win/win negotiation skills. I asked Tyler why he was unwilling to change his pants. He said that friends of his were going to be at the lecture. Everyone who was "cool" wears holes in their jeans and he wanted to be "cool," too. I explained my position: "It's important for you to win. I want you to win. However, I will be embarrassed in front of all these people if you have holes in your jeans. How can I win, too?"

I couldn't think of a solution, but Tyler thought for a moment and said, "How about this? How about if I wear a good pair of pants over my jeans? Then, when I'm around your friends, I won't have holes. When I'm around my friends, I'll take them off." I marveled at Tyler's creativity. I said, "What a great solution! I would have never thought of that. Thanks for negotiating with me."

To summarize, when you are in the middle of a power struggle with your child and negotiation seems like the appropriate tool, ask your child, "I see how you can win and that's great, because I want you to win. How can I win, too?" When children see that you're just as interested in their winning, they're eager to help figure out ways that you both can have what you want.

Make it okay for a child to do what she wants

Sometimes you just can't get your children to do, or not do, something, no matter how hard you try. If you find yourself facing such a situation, think for a moment about the possibility that what they want could be acceptable, after all. If you can legitimize their activity, you will eliminate the power struggle. Think creatively, as this parent and this teacher did:

A mother of four children could not get her children to quit writing graffiti on the walls, no matter what discipline strategies she used. So she wallpapered the children's bathroom with white wallpaper and told them that they could write whatever they wanted in their bathroom. When they were given permission to do that, they confined their drawings to the bathroom, much to Mom's relief! Whenever I went to their house, I would use the kids' bathroom because it was the most interesting room in the house!

↻

A teacher had a problem in her classroom with the pilot makers of paper airplanes. They turned the classroom into a busy airport! She decided to make a bad situation a learning opportunity and devoted some time in the classroom to the study of aerodynamics. As part of the curriculum, the children had to make paper airplanes that demonstrated the best aerodynamic designs. Much to her amazement, the students' fascination with paper planes dwindled.

Teach your child how to say "No" respectfully

Some power struggles occur because children have not been taught how to say "No" respectfully. Most of us were raised to do as our parents told us, whether we liked it or not. However, children who aren't allowed to say "No" directly say it indirectly. They can say it by dawdling, forgetting, or doing a job ineffectively so that you either have to finish it for them or you don't bother to ask them again. Some children even get sick. It is much more difficult to deal with a "No" that is said "under the table" than one said directly. If a child can say "No" directly, his communication is honest and clear. How many times have you gotten yourself in trouble because you felt you couldn't say "No"? Allowing your children to say it won't cost you anything because they are already saying it indirectly.

Think of the benefits for a child who can say "No." He can say it to peers who want him to participate in drugs, sex, stealing, vandalism, hurtful activity, and other situations where someone wishes to coerce him. If you don't teach your children, who will? The pressure to be liked by parents early in a child's life is probably equivalent to the peer pressure they will feel as a teen, so what a great time to learn and practice saying "No"!

In our family, everyone is allowed to say "No." We respect the desire of the person who says it. We also have an agreement that if someone says, "But it's really important that XYZ happens," then the person who says "No" will be willing to negotiate. Remember that negotiation means each person gets what he or she wants.

For example, I may ask my child to help clean up the house.

Sometimes he'll say, "No, I don't want to," and that won't be okay with me. At those times, I say, "But it's important to me to get the house picked up because we're having friends over tonight." So we negotiate a win/win solution. Tyler might say, "I'll watch Brianna [his three-year-old sister] for you, instead." Then I have the free time to clean up. We both win.

As odd as it sounds, when you allow your children to say "No," they are more willing to cooperate. You have given them power in the situation and that makes them feel they have some control.

How would you feel if you were in a job or a relationship in which you weren't allowed to say "No?" I know I would become resentful. In fact, I would probably leave the situation if there were nothing I could do to change it. Our children often leave emotionally, even if they can't leave physically, by becoming distant and uncommunicative.

One of the best ways to teach your child how to say "No" is to model saying it yourself. Your "No" may also be phrased as "I'm unwilling to . . . " This is how one mother modeled saying "No" to her children:

Two children wanted to get a pet rabbit. Mom told them, "I am willing to pay for a rabbit's food. I'm unwilling to feed a rabbit, clean its cage, or clean up its messes. If you miss feeding the rabbit or taking care of it for two days in a row, I will take the rabbit back to the pet store."

Be careful that you don't say "No" in an angry way. An angry tone of voice indicates displeasure, disapproval, and sometimes punishment to a child. You want to model that saying "No" is a normal, everyday sort of activity—no different in degree than saying "Yes," or, "The sky is blue today."

Sometimes, parents try to postpone disappointing children with phrases like "I'll see," or "Maybe," or "Let me think about it." This behavior doesn't model saying "No" effectively to a child. The child gives up asking after a while. The parent is off the hook, but the result is a discouraged child.) If we say "No" in a kind, but firm tone of voice (and offer a reason when possible), our children will respect us and learn how to say it themselves.

Ways to avoid power struggles

Slow down

A major reason for power struggles today is over-scheduling of time. The more we rush and are anxious to get things done, the more we put pressure on our children to do things quickly. Children are not developmentally ready to do everything quickly or in an organized manner. The more we pressure them, the more resistant they become. This creates tension in families, and tension is a fertile breeding ground for power struggles and tantrums. Allow yourself enough time so that you don't have to hurry your child. Slow down—there isn't time to rush!

Plan ahead

You can avoid last minute pressure by planning ahead. For example, have your child get school clothes, books, lunch, etc. ready the night before. While everyone is calm, you can discuss what clothes will be worn, whether homework is finished and organized; see if there is enough lunch meat for sandwiches or find out if you're expected to supply cupcakes; and discuss what everyone will be doing during the week so you can avoid conflicts. Children are more cooperative and pleasant when they can go at their own pace, and they know what to expect.

Make agreements ahead of time

Do you go crazy when you get into the store and your child wants to buy candy and toys? Or when you have run an errand with your child and the minute you get where you need to be she starts whining to leave? An effective way to deal with this kind of problem is to make an agreement with your child ahead of time. The determining factor for success in making agreements is that you keep your word. If you don't keep your word, your child will learn to distrust you and refuse to cooperate.

A mom owned her own business and would frequently take her child with her to work. Mother made an agreement ahead of time with her child, "We will be here for only fifteen minutes, and then we will go." Her daughter would sit and draw while Mom worked.

Eventually, Mom began to stretch the fifteen minutes because her child was playing so happily. The little girl figured out that they were staying later and later. She started putting up quite a fuss when Mom wanted to take her to the office. When Mom realized what was happening, she began to honor her commitment to leave at the agreed-upon time. Her daughter gradually became more willing to go to work with her again.

If you plan on going shopping, tell your child ahead of time how much money you're willing to spend on him. Tell him that you're unwilling spend any more than that amount. It works best to actually give him the money. Design a consequence for what happens if he bugs you to buy more than the designated amount. One possibility is that the next time when you go shopping he will have to stay home. In today's society, it's all too easy for your child to misinterpret commercials and advertisements that lead to the belief, "Love means that my parents' buying things and my having things will make me happy." Such a belief can create power struggles between you.

Give notice of time

You've been invited to a special party for a visiting dignitary. There are many interesting people to talk to, and you're circulating from one stimulating group of people to another. You haven't had so much fun in years! You settle into a conversation with a woman from Russia who is telling you about their social customs. Suddenly, your husband grabs your hand, forces your coat on you, and says, "Come on. It's time to go home."

How would you feel? What would you feel like doing? Children have similar feelings when we demand that they make an abrupt shift in what they're doing (like going home from a friend's house or going to bed). You will have fewer power struggles if you give them a friendly warning, such as, "We will be leaving in five minutes," or, "Bedtime is in ten minutes. I'll set the timer." Notice how much better you would have felt toward your husband if he had said in the above example, "I would like to leave in 15 minutes."

To avoid conflict, we sometimes don't tell our children about changes in plans until the last minute. This makes our child feel out of control and can lead to power struggles. For example, I used to tell my children the day before I had to go out of town. They were usually disappointed, and reacted angrily. I now tell my children about trips at our family meeting at the beginning of the week. This allows us to plan a special date together before I leave. As a result, my children have been less upset about my leaving.

Do the unexpected

Children generally have their parents' reactions to almost everything figured out at a very early age. They know what to expect. When you do the unexpected, your child no longer gets your usual response to that behavior. As a result, you break the pattern of the power struggle.

Richard had an ongoing power struggle with his kids about slamming doors in the house. After trying many ways to get them to stop, he decided to do the unexpected. One weekend, without saying another word, he took all the doors the kids had been slamming off their hinges. Richard told his wife, "They can't slam doors that don't exist." Three days later, he put the doors back up. There was no more door slamming. In fact, when visiting children would slam a door, Richard would overhear his kids tell the offenders, "Around here, we don't slam doors."

We continue to try to correct behavior with the same ineffective methods we've always used and wonder why we have no success. If we just changed our pattern by doing the unexpected once in a while, the misbehavior would often change permanently. Ask yourself, "What do I normally do in this situation? Would this be an appropriate time to do the unexpected?"

Make discipline fun

Many of us approach discipline (teaching) far too seriously. Think about how much more you learn when you're enjoying yourself.

Make life's lessons fun for you and your child. For example, try singing "No" instead of speaking in your usual admonishing voice or try developing a funny character (perhaps Donald Duck) that makes requests to do things, such as household chores.

I was struggling with Tyler over his homework. He was supposed to be learning the multiplication tables, and we were getting nowhere fast! Finally, I asked Tyler, "When you're learning something, do you need to see it, hear it, or feel it?" He said that he needed all three ways. So I took out an oblong cake pan and put a layer of his father's shaving cream in the bottom. I wrote the problem in the shaving cream and Tyler wrote the answer. I was amazed! He went from a child who couldn't care less about what nine times seven equaled to a child who was rapidly writing the answers with as much glee as if he were let loose in a toy store. And, of course, the homework session ended in an uproarious shaving cream fight between us.

You may think you don't have time to come up with unique ways for your child to learn, or that you aren't creative. I urge you to throw these self-limiting thoughts out the window. The shaving cream technique was not only an easy way to help Tyler learn, but it also became a close bonding time for both of us. It certainly was better than the "pulling teeth" method of multiplication drill.

One mom was having a power struggle with her small son over his bath. As usual, no end to the struggle was in sight. She noticed two squirt guns in her son's bedroom. Grabbing the squirt guns, she yelled invitingly, "Let's have a squirt-gun fight in the bathtub!" Both had a great time laughing in the tub, and Mom accomplished her goal.

Maybe your children are too old for this particular bath technique, but the purpose of the example is to stretch your imagination. Make parenting more fun for you and your child in as many ways as you can think of. While you're defusing power struggles in the present, you're also creating memories of family fun for the future.

Withdraw from the conflict

Children frequently attempt to defy us. Some parents respond to a child's defiant behavior by trying to force him to behave or to take "the wind out of his sails." Instead, "take your sails out of his wind." You have nothing to lose by withdrawing from conflict and potentially much to gain once you have time and space to think about a solution. Even if you succeed in overpowering your child, he will ultimately feel hurt. As a result, he will try to hurt you back. He may not be capable of hurting you physically, but he'll find other ways, such as doing poorly in school, forgetting chores, "accidently" causing damage to possessions or property, or some other indirect misbehavior.

Since it takes two to fight, refuse to participate in power struggles with a child. When you find yourself in a conflict, and you feel that it's escalating instead of resolving, withdraw from the conflict. Remember, words said in anger can be very destructive and slow to fade from memory.

A mother was in her car, about to leave the shopping center with her son. He had asked her to buy him a toy and she had said, "No." He continued asking her why she wouldn't buy him the toy. She explained that she didn't want to spend her money on a toy that day. But, he kept picking at her to buy the toy. Mom noticed that she was losing her patience and was about to explode. Instead, she got out of the car (she took her keys with her) and sat on the hood. She waited there for a few minutes until she cooled off. When she got back in the car, her son asked her, "What's the matter?" Mom said, "Sometimes I get angry when you won't take "No" for an answer. I like how determined you are and I would also like you to just take "No" for an answer sometimes." This unexpected, but honest, exchange impressed her son. As a result, he began to accept it when she said, "No."

Know your child

Knowing your child will help you determine which intervention to use when your child is about to have a temper tantrum. For example, when Tyler is overtired, he gets really irritable and sometimes mean. I know that my best bet at this point is to dispense with any discipline or negotiation and encourage him to go to bed as soon as possible.

Watch how your child acts in different situations. When your

child gets hungry or tired, does she become irritable and less cooperative? Which children does she play best with? Does she play
better at someone else's house? Or does she play better in neutral
territory such as a park where she does not feel she has to protect
her territory? How long can she play with another child before she
starts needing her own space? When your teenager comes home
from school, is it best to allow him some time before you discuss his
day? Or does he respond better right before bedtime?

Watch your child's patterns to know when your child is really
"misbehaving" or just physically uncomfortable.

It is much more helpful if you can get your child's basic needs
met as quickly as possible rather than getting into power struggles.

Signals

For the parent and child who want to work on power struggles
together and are cooperative enough in their relationship, signals
they devise between themselves can help. Signals are a tool to alert
the other person that a power struggle is beginning.

Use discrete signals so that no one is humiliated or embarrassed
by them. It's best if you let your child create the signal. However,
make sure that you both have agreed on it and feel comfortable
using it. Signals that are funny are also a light way of helping each
other. They can be either verbal or nonverbal. Here is an example:

*One mom and daughter found that they had too many angry outbursts,
so they decided they would have a secret signal to alert the other that a power
struggle was beginning. They decided pulling an ear lobe (their own, of course)
would be a discreet reminder to the other person that she was using anger to get
her way. Then they would choose a better way to solve their problem.*

*One family realized they were saying discouraging things to each other,
which often led to verbal power struggles. So they developed the phrase,
"That's a put down," as a signal. Everyone in the family agreed that when*

*they heard the signal they would start using more encouraging phrases imme-
diately.*

↻

*A mother got tired of the ordeal of planning family outings only to have
someone ruin them with their bad attitude (including herself). So the family
decided to use a signal to help keep from struggling to make each other stop
being negative. Anyone could yell, "Attitude!" when they heard someone
expressing a bad attitude. Then the family would gather together with their
thumbs up in the center of a circle. The family would then shout, "One, two,
three . . . Out of here!" as they simultaneously raised their thumbs over
their heads. The phrase, of course, meant that the attitude was to leave, not
the individual. [This funny exercise will backfire if parents don't acknowledge
their own bad attitudes, also.]*

The goal of revenge

The child who is extremely discouraged may openly–physically or
emotionally–hurt herself or others. When we overpower children,
they become discouraged and resort to the goal of revenge. Feeling worthless, disliked, and hurt by others, these children want to
hurt back in the same way they feel they've been hurt.

As with other goals of children's misbehavior, use your own
feelings as your guide to your child's intent. When you feel hurtful
or revengeful toward your child, it's a good indication that his goal
is revenge for some hurt he has suffered.

*Ten-year-old Terri got caught stealing fifty cents from a boy at school,
and the teacher sent a note to her parents. Terri's mother was livid. "Terri,
how could you do this to us? We would have given you the money. I'm
ashamed of you. You have given us nothing but trouble. I just don't understand you. Now, you go to your room. I don't want to see or hear from you
until you're sorry for what you've done." Mom gave her a swat on her bottom
and sent Terri to her room.*

Later that evening, Terri decided to paint her fingernails even though

Mom had told her not to play with nail polish. As she was finishing her nails, she "accidentally" spilled the nail polish remover all over Mom's antique table, taking the finish off as she tried to clean it up.

Redirecting the goal of revenge

It takes patience and understanding to see behind your child's hurtfulness. It might help to know that sometimes her hatefulness reflects her own feelings about herself.

It's important for you to decide that you will end the war and that you will be the first one to stop hurting back. This is difficult to do because we feel so justified in wanting to hurt back or in wanting to teach the child a lesson. But ask yourself whether you want peace or war. If you decide you're unwilling to quit the war just yet, it's okay. Just realize that your attempts to discipline will be increasingly less effective.

If you choose peace, take these five steps to redirect the goal of revenge:

1. **Stop all hurtful actions, words, and punishment.** If we retaliate, even though we may temporarily subdue our child's misbehavior, we will only aggravate the problem. Punishment gives him justification for continued aggression—direct or indirect. You won't solve the problem by avoiding retaliation, but neither will you continue to make it worse.

2. **List five things you love about your child.** You may find it difficult to think about things you love about the child who is hurting you when you feel angry. However, your attitude about your child will change from negative to more hopeful, and possibly even positive. When you have a positive attitude, it is easier to create effective solutions than when you are angry or hurt.

3. **Protect yourself from getting hurt.** Sometimes we stay in a situation that is hurtful to us, hoping that things will get bet-

ter. Usually if you stay in such a situation, you end up feeling hurt and resentful, and even suffering injury.

A sixteen-year-old boy specialized in frequent obscenities directed at his mother. Usually, she would try to make him stop talking to her like that, which only escalated the problem. She decided to protect herself by leaving the room the minute he started to say hurtful things to her.

4. **Make amends to the child.** Sometimes, it's difficult to admit you were wrong or to say honestly that you're sorry. Other times, we feel someone else is at fault, and so we aren't going to say we're sorry until the other person does first. Remember, you're the adult in this situation and your child is learning about relationships from you. Model the behavior you wish your child to learn.

   Your child may be so mad at you that he won't allow you to make amends or repair your relationship. This child may need time. You may want to say, "I can see that you still want to hurt me. If you need time to be mad at me, it's okay with me. I'll wait."

5. **Reestablish a loving relationship with your child.** Do something to repair the relationship. Go on a date; do something fun together. The purpose is for you to get close again. Do not buy him things to assuage your guilt.

In more extreme cases of revenge, there may not be any relationship with him because you are both so hurtful to one another that you don't feel like being in the other's presence. In this case, it's important that the whole family see a therapist or counselor.

Terri's mother recognized that she had hurt Terri and made her feel unloved by the things she had said. For two days after the nail polish incident, Mother said nothing about the damaged table. She avoided hurting or punishing Terri. She also spent time thinking about some things she enjoyed about her daughter and mentioned a few of those things to Terri. After the two-day cooling-off period, Mother talked to Terri about the incident. "I must have hurt you when I said that you were nothing but trouble. Sometimes I say hurtful things when I don't know what else to do. I'm sorry, and I've decided to make a centerpiece to cover the spot on the table. Would you like to help me make it?"

Because of this mother's understanding and her determination to end the battle of revenge between the two of them, mother and daughter were able to enjoy each other's company as they worked on a project together.

When you recognize the goal of revenge, use only natural consequences until you establish a better relationship. Natural and logical consequences are described in Chapter 7. A child who is looking for an excuse to get even may easily misinterpret a logical consequence as punishment. Don't confront this child when you're angry. He can sense your anger and may use it against you.

Teenage Aaron was supposed to be studying. Instead, he was painting a banner for an after-school club. This was a source of iritation to his mother because she had been in an ongoing battle with him about homework since school began. Mom started nagging her son. "You promised you'd do your homework before you did anything else. How come you aren't keeping your word?" Aaron didn't even bother looking up from the banner. "I will. Now will you quit bugging me?" His mother gave a sarcastic laugh, "Yeah, I've heard that one before. I want you to stop what you're doing now and finish your homework. You'll never amount to anything!" Her son stood up and threw the brush down on the banner and shouted, "Why don't you just leave me alone, you @*#? I'll do my homework when I'm ready. I'm sick of you telling me what to do!" He stormed into his bedroom and slammed the door.

His mother realized that Aaron was feeling revengeful. She decided to be the first of the two to stop the battle. First, she remembered the step of doing something to reestablish their relationship. She let the situation cool down, and later asked him to come out of his room. She offered to help him paint the banner and he agreed. They talked together freely for the first time in months. The next morning, Aaron got up early and finished his homework.

Here are two exercises you can do if you have a particularly difficult child. The first thing you can do is to visualize how you want the relationship to be. Take five minutes in the morning before you start your day and five minutes at night before you fall asleep to visualize your relationship. Actually see the images and hear the words that you want each of you to say. Create the feeling you would like to have when you are around this child.

Parents often imagine the worst possible outcomes for their children—the son gets in an accident or the daughter uses drugs, and so on. Instead of imagining these possibilities, imagine the possibilities you would most like to see. You may or may not achieve success right away in visualizing these, but be patient.

The second thing you can do with a difficult child is to practice loving him unconditionally. Remember when he was little, it was even okay if he threw up on your brand new clothes, you loved him anyway! Try practicing loving him unconditionally for a day and if a day is too long, practice for an hour a day.

Halfway through her senior year in high school, seventeen-year-old Tracy decided to leave home and live in an apartment on her own. Her mother gave her a gas credit card with the understanding that Tracy would be responsible for paying all the bills on the card. Mom got a call from the credit card company warning her that someone had charged $800 on the card in a very short period. Mom got her card back from Tracy and made arrangements for her daughter to pay back the $800.

Mom said that she was really tempted not to give her daughter any Christmas presents because she was so angry. However, Mom knew that such an action would come out of her wish to get revenge, to punish her daughter. She would not improve the situation, even though she was very tempted to get back at her daughter.

Three things happened in this incident: first, Mom stayed unconditionally loving; second, Mom did not punish her daughter by taking away her presents; and third, Mom stood up for her rights by taking back the card and arranging for Tracy to pay the charges.

Sometimes, extrinsic circumstances lead a child to the goal of revenge. He may be feeling overpowered by a parent, sibling, or someone at school. This child may have a physical limitation, illness, or learning disorder which he feels angry about because he can't do things the way others do. Sometimes, children who have not bonded well with their parents will seek revenge.

Here is an example of how a mother dealt with revenge directed at her though she was not the source of the child's desire for revenge:

Nathan started yelling, seemingly for no reason, at his mother when she requested something from him. Mom asked, "Did I do something to hurt you?" After much conversation, she found out that Nathan was letting a friend of his intimidate him. Nathan tended to be unassertive and not very confident about himself. They decided to enroll him in an Aikido class. Gradually, his self-confidence improved, and the problem was solved.

The goal of avoidance

Children who feel like they can't do anything or can't meet the demands life makes on them resort to avoiding everything, whether it's challenging or easy.

Angie's parents had noticed that she was withdrawing more and more from family activities. Her tone of voice was becoming whiny and she would start crying with the slightest provocation. When asked to participate in activities, she would frequently whimper, "I can't." She also started mumbling words so that it was difficult to understand her. Her parents became extremely concerned about her behavior at home and at school.

Angie began displaying the goal of avoidance. She had become so discouraged that she was giving up. It was as if she were saying, "I'm helpless and useless. Don't make any demands on me. Leave me alone." Children with this goal exaggerate their weaknesses, and they frequently convince us that they are dumb or clumsy. Our initial reaction or response may be to feel sorry for them. You rarely reprimand this child. At times you might feel frustrated because nothing seems to work. Some parents react with irritation to their child's helplessness.

Redirecting the goal of avoidance

Here are the steps to redirect this behavior:

1. **Stop feeling that she is not capable.** Do not feel sorry her, coax her, or make fewer demands on her than you do on other children. When we feel sorry for our children, we encourage self-pity and convince them that we don't have faith in them, that we agree with their belief about themselves. There is nothing that paralyzes anyone more than feeling sorry for herself. If we help a child do something we know she can do for herself, she will get what she wants by being sad. When this habit is carried into adulthood, we call it depression.

2. **Start changing your expectations about your child.** Concentrate on what the child has accomplished. Start seeing your child as capable. Talk about what she can do; don't discuss what she hasn't done.

3. **Be understanding, but don't feel sorry for her.** For example, "You seem to feel like you can't do that," versus "Here, let me do that for you. It's too hard for you, isn't it?"

4. **Make her helplessness inappropriate.** Suppose she says she can't do something that you know she can do. Say to her, "Do it anyway," in a loving tone of voice.

5. **Arrange situations or activities in which the child can succeed.** Start with easy things you know she can do and gradually increase the difficulty of the activities as her confidence increases.

Eight-year-old Liz avoided her schoolwork. Long after a math assignment had been given, the teacher noticed that Liz had not even started the assignment. The teacher asked Liz why. Liz replied meekly, "I can't." The teacher asked, "What part of the assignment would you be willing to do?" Liz shrugged her shoulders. The teacher asked, "Would you be willing to write your name?" Liz agreed and the teacher left for a few moments.

Liz wrote her name, but nothing else. The teacher then asked Liz if she would be willing to do the next two problems, and Liz agreed. This continued until Liz had completed most of the assignment. The teacher had arranged for small successes for Liz by breaking the assignment down into manageable tasks.

↻

Kevin, a nine-year-old boy, was given the assignment of looking up spelling words in the dictionary and then writing out the meanings. His father noticed that Kevin did all he could to avoid his homework. He cried and whined and told his father that he felt stupid. Dad realized that Kevin felt overwhelmed by the project and was defeating himself before he even tried. So Dad decided to break the task down into something that was more manageable for Kevin.

For the first three weeks, Dad looked up the words and Kevin wrote down the meanings. Then Dad also had Kevin look up the first letter of the word in the dictionary. Dad then alternated looking up every other word with Kevin. Dad continued to break down the task until Kevin could successfully do the whole task without his help. The process took several months to complete. It proved to be very helpful to Kevin in his school work and in his relationship with his dad.

Be sincere about all encouragement you offer children who feel defeated and inadequate. Such children will be extremely sensitive and suspicious of encouragement and may try to discount it.

Children's Mistaken Goals

Parent's feelings:
- Annoyed with child
- Want to remind or coax child
- Feel delighted with "good" child

Child's reactions to reprimand:
- Temporarily stops misbehavior when given attention

Child's action seems to say:
- "I only count when I'm noticed or being served."
- "I believe being loved equals having attention."

Child's goal is likely to be:
- ATTENTION

Parental corrective action:
- Make no eye contact.
- Do not speak to child.
- Make child feel loved (without words).
- Take action as soon as child annoys you.
- Teach child to get attention appropriately.

Parent's feelings:
- Provoked with child
- Feel need for power
- Challenged by child (Parent thinks, "I'll make you do it!" or, "You can't get away with that!")

Child's reaction to reprimand:
- Intensifies misbehavior
- Wants to be the boss; wants to win

Child's action seems to say:
- "I only count when I'm dominating you."
- "I only count when you do what I want you to do."
- "I only count when I prove that you can't boss me."

Child's goal is likely to be:
- POWER

Parental corrective action:
- Give choices, not orders.
- Don't play "tug-of-war."
- Give friendly eye contact.
- Don't fight and don't give in.
- Give child useful ways to feel powerful.
- Teach child to win/win negotiate.

Parent's feelings:

- Hurt; angry
- Revengeful
- Thinks, "How could you do this to me?"

Child's reaction to reprimand:

- Wants to get even
- Makes others dislike him or her

Child's action seems to say:

- "I can hurt others as I have been hurt."

Child's goal is likely to be:

- REVENGE

Parental corrective action:

- Do not hurt back.
- Reestablish the relationship.
- Use logical consequences the child will enjoy.
- Make amends if you are wrong.
- Teach child to assert feelings of hurt in appropriate ways.

Parent's feelings:

- Despair
- Annoyed and sorry for child
- Thinks, "What can I do?"

Child's reaction to reprimand:

- No reaction because no reprimand was given.
- Feels there is no use in trying.
- Passive

Child's action seems to say:

- "I can't do anything right, so I won't do anything at all."
- "I'm no good."
- "Leave me alone."

Child's goal is likely to be:

- AVOIDANCE

Parental corrective action:

- Don't coax or feel sorry for child.
- Arrange for success in small, manageable steps.
- Avoid doing things for child.
- Find or create situations in which child can feel valuable.
- Teach child to feel capable by overcoming obstacles and accomplishing tasks.

(Adapted from an original chart by Nancy Pearcy and Louise Van Vilet)

Practice identifying goals of misbehavior

Read the examples, then answer the four questions that follow each one. The answers are on page 119.

Mary starts tapping her pencil on her desk. The teacher asks her to stop, but the tapping continues. The teacher snaps at Mary, "I said to stop that!" Mary retorts, "No, I won't, and you can't make me!"

    1. How does the teacher feel?
    2. What was Mary's reaction to her reprimand?
    3. What did Mary's behavior seem to be saying?
    4. What would you guess is Mary's goal?

Mary starts tapping her pencil during class. The teacher says, "Mary." Mary stops immediately and says, "I'm sorry, Teacher. Do you want me to say all the ABCs now?" "Not now, Mary," the teacher responds. "Wait until your turn." "But I know all of them. Please, can I say them?" "Well, all right," concedes the teacher. "Aaa . . . Beee . . . Ceee . . ." Mary's teacher sighs and rolls her eyes as Mary slowly says the alphabet.

    1. How does the teacher feel?
    2. What was Mary's reaction to her reprimand?
    3. What did Mary's behavior seem to be saying?
    4. What would you guess is Mary's goal?

During class, Mary suddenly slams her hand down on the desk and jumps to her feet, saying, "This is stupid going over the ABCs. I learned them a long time ago!" The teacher is shocked. She responds by curtly telling Mary, "I'll not have you talking to me that way, young lady. I'm sending a note home to your mother." "Big deal," Mary retorts. "That does it!" says

the teacher sharply. "You're going down to the principal's office!"

1. How does the teacher feel?
2. What was Mary's reaction to her reprimand?
3. What did Mary's behavior seem to be saying?
4. What would you guess is Mary's goal?

During class, the teacher calls on Mary to say the alphabet. Mary says, "I don't know it" and looks down at her feet. "Come on now, Mary," the teacher coaxes, "I know you can say it." Mary shrugs her shoulders. The teacher sighs, then in a gentle voice says, "Come on, Mary, can you say the first letter? Can you say "A?" Mary weakly says, "A." "That's good, Mary," the teacher praises.

1. How does the teacher feel?
2. What was Mary's reaction to her reprimand?
3. What did Mary's behavior seem to be saying?
4. What would you guess is Mary's goal?

Answers, in order of the examples:

1. Teacher feels angry. Her authority has been challenged.
2. The reprimand was ignored.
3. "You can't make me."
4. Power.

1. Teacher feels annoyed.
2. Misbehavior stops because child received attention.
3. "Notice me."
4. Attention.

I. Teacher feels hurt and revengeful. Feels like hurting back.
2. Mary hurts the teacher again after the reprimand.
3. "I want to hurt others the way I feel hurt."
4. Revenge.

1. Teacher feels annoyed and sympathetic.
2. No reprimand was given.
3. "Leave me alone."
4. Avoidance, inadequacy.

7

Discipline
that Teaches
Self-Control

E ffective discipline methods are an integral part of redirecting children's behavior. If you often use the techniques of punishment and rewards, you should know that they are ineffective methods of preparing children for democratic living. Three essential elements are missing—a sense of responsibility, a feeling of mutual respect, and the ability to cooperate. Trade in those methods for ones that teach inner control and self-responsibility.

Guidelines for parental behavior

Before we discuss the three discipline methods themselves (self-quieting, limits, and consequences), some general guidelines for parent behavior are in order. They are: work on one problem at a time; balance firmness and kindness; talk about your problem, not theirs; concentrate on what you can do; respect your hang-ups; refrain from making children suffer as they learn; and choose to be close to your children.

Work on one problem at a time

It's important to work on one problem at a time so that you and your child don't become overwhelmed or discouraged. When you solve one problem, you will often find that others clear up because they were related to it.

Balance firmness and kindness

The key to effectiveness is a balance of firmness and kindness. Some parents are too kind (permissive) and some are too firm (domineering). Some are both kind and firm, but not at the same time. What works is to combine both qualities into each interaction.

You combine kindness and firmness when you:

- accept and love your child as she is

- do not make your child suffer

- do not rescue her from uncomfortable situations she creates for herself

- do not allow her to infringe on your rights

- take action when misbehavior persists

Mom made an agreement with her children that they could eat in front of the television as long as they cleaned up their mess. The children would for-

get, and Mom usually would spend a lot of time yelling at them.

What Mother needs to do is pick up the food silently and return it to the kitchen. She may want to say in a firm and friendly voice, "Since you broke your agreement about cleaning up your mess, I'm unwilling to have you eat here now. You can try again tomorrow." At this point, the children might try to get her to respond in her old way, by yelling at them but still letting them continue to eat in front of the television.

Parents either give in or get angry when children begin to complain. It is important that you neither argue nor explain. If you argue, you are initiating a power struggle; if you explain, you are giving attention (and they already know why you object). Instead, give your children a look of acceptance, or some other friendly gesture, and say nothing. If they persist, you leave the room.

Talk about your problem, not the child's

Essential to effective discipline is the requirement that you talk about your problem, not the child's. This approach makes your child feel less defensive because you aren't sticking your nose in his business. Say, "I'm unwilling to have a messy living room," instead of, "You must pick up your stuff." Model self-respect. This maximizes your chance of winning his cooperation. Here is an experience I had with my husband:

My husband was sitting in the living room reading. I had gone to bed. After a few minutes, I called out to him, "Honey, you have to get up early in the morning, so you'd better not stay up too long." He answered, "Okay, okay," his tone of voice revealing that he didn't appreciate my nagging. About fifteen minutes later, I asked, "Are you going to read much longer?" He snapped back at me, saying, "I told you, I don't know how long I'm going to read!" At that point, he was determined to read all night!

I changed my approach. Instead of trying to make him feel that I was concerned about him, I talked about my problem. I said, "I have to get up early tomorrow, and when you come to bed late, it wakes me up. Would you be willing to come to bed now and read in bed, or would you be willing to sleep in the guest room when you're finished reading?" He reacted quite differently.

He said, "It's not so important that I read right now. I'll come to bed."

Parents mislead children when they concentrate on the kids' problems. The kids get the idea that as long as Mom or Dad are willing to take responsibility for the kids' problems, they don't need to do anything themselves.

Here are three examples that show how most of us have been accustomed to speaking to our children (or how our parents spoke to us). Following each statement is a suggested alternative that models self-respect.

Old	New
"I don't want you watching television until all hours of the evening."	"After 9 p.m. I would like the living room to myself."

Old	New
"Stop that fighting right now! You'll get hurt."	"I'm unwilling to risk damage to my things by allowing you to fight in the house."

Old	New
"It's time for you to get a job. You must learn to be more responsible."	"I need your help to make ends meet, and would like you to start buying your own clothes."

Before you start to model self-respecting talk, ask yourself, "What is my problem in this situation? What do I seek a solution for?" Remember that you are addressing *your* problem.

Concentrate on what you can do

Parents issue several hundred commands to their children each day. These sound like, "Get up. It's time for school. Get dressed. Eat your breakfast. Put your dishes away. Brush your teeth. Brush your hair. Don't forget your homework. Put your shoes on. Pick up your toys. Turn off the TV. Come here," and more. With such a constant harangue, wouldn't you turn a deaf ear? The commands may be given in a threatening tone of voice, also. Imagine if your boss spoke that way to you. My guess is you would quickly be looking for a new job. Fortunately, our children can't go looking for a new family. Nor can they always express how they feel verbally, so feelings show up in their behavior. They resist, dawdle, or forget; sometimes they actually put their hands over their ears to shut us out physically.

During conflicts, most of us become defensive and address what someone else should do, instead of what we can do. Stop and ask yourself, "What can I do?" when this happens to you. By controlling your own actions rather than someone else's, you can influence their behavior without disturbing the good relationship you have with them.

Instead of talking so much, take friendly action. Give your child his comb or his toothbrush with toothpaste on it. Guide your child to his task by gently and lovingly placing a hand on his back.

Mother was tired of nagging and reminding her children to set the table every night. She decided to take some action. That evening, she put the food on the table, sat down, and silently waited. The kids came in and asked, "What are we waiting for, Mom?" At that point, Mother could have lectured, "We wouldn't have to wait if you had done what I've told you to do a hundred times!" Instead, she very briefly and casually answered, "Silverware and plates." The kids rushed off and came back with the silverware and dishes.

Another mother, whose children never picked up their dirty clothes without being nagged, stated simply, "From now on, I'll wash only clothes that are in the hamper." She then took action by not washing clothes left out of the hamper. Her children understood the message and made sure dirty clothes made it to the hamper.

Both mothers quit nagging and reminding, which helped them to feel better about themselves and their children. When we spend less time being negative, we can enjoy our children a lot more.

Respect your hang-ups

Even when it's your child's responsibility to be concerned about her problems, not yours, parents have personal hang-ups. For example, if your teenager stays out late and doesn't get enough sleep, that's her problem, right? If you have a hang-up about her safety, you have a right to relief, however. You have the right to say, "I know you can handle any situation that comes up, but I have this hang-up. When you're out after 11 p.m., I worry. I don't know if something has happened to you. I'm not sure if I should call the police or wait. Do you have any suggestions about what I could do about my problem?" Another way of saying this is, "Even though I have a hang-up about this, I would like you to respect how I feel."

If you say to your teenager, "You must be home by 11 p.m. on weekend nights so you'll get enough sleep," your daughter will probably tune you out.

Children don't need to suffer to learn

In the past, parents believed that children needed to suffer if they were to remember to do something differently. Many of us believe this, too, often subconsciously, and it affects our tone of voice and gestures when we discipline children.

A father and his son were in an automobile accident. The father was killed instantly. The boy, who was seriously injured, was rushed to the hospital. A doctor washed up, walked into the operating room, looked at the boy, and exclaimed, "I can't operate on this boy. He's my son!"

How do you explain this? The answer is the doctor was the boy's mother. Our subconscious belief might make us assume the doctor was a man. If I had asked you, "Do you believe all doctors are men?" you would probably have answered, "Of course not." But your subconscious belief, and not your common sense, supplied the first answer.

Likewise, when we discipline children, we often operate from our subconscious belief that children must suffer in order to learn.

There was a boy in summer camp whose mother asked for help. Her son refused to wash his hands before meals. She was quite irritated by this. When the child arrived at camp, I said to him in a friendly tone of voice, "Tom, it's your business if you wash your hands or not, but when you come to the table with dirty hands, you pass germs around. I don't want to get sick. So, unless you have a better idea, from now on I will only serve people who come to the table with clean hands."

That very afternoon Tom put me to the test by coming to the table with dirt on his hands. I calmly reached across the table and removed his plate. Do you know what that kid did? He sat right across from me and smiled through the whole meal. I was boiling inside! He appeared not to care that he wasn't eating. Finally, in a gruff voice I said, "You know, you're not getting anything to eat until dinner time!"

I said the wrong thing! The outcome of his behavior had become a punishment. I was now involved in the same power struggle he had with his mother. The thing that got me into trouble was, without being consciously aware of it, I believed that if Tom didn't suffer, he wouldn't learn.

When your child sees your intent is not to make her suffer, she'll become more cooperative.

Choose closeness with your child

Concentrate on developing closeness in your relationship with your child. Don't concern yourself with who is "right" or "wrong" or whether or not you're in control. The top priority should be to understand your feelings and your child's feelings. The choices you make to redirect your child's behavior will be more appropriate and effective. The application of rules where there is no relationship results in rebellion. Ask yourself, "Do I want to be right, in control, or close?"

Self-quieting

Time-out is a common discipline tool that becomes punishment when a parent uses it in an angry manner and as a way to control her child. For example, "I'm sick and tired of your whining! Go to your room and stay there until you can behave!" Notice that the parent is sending her child away in anger. The message her child receives is, "I don't like you. I want you to go away." When the parent is in control of when her child comes out of her room, the child does not learn self-control. When time-out is seen as punishment, the child feels resentful. She doesn't think about what to do differently in the future. Instead, her thoughts are, "This is stupid! I'm angry! Mom isn't fair!" Time-out loses its effectiveness when it becomes punishment. Self-quieting, on the other hand, teaches internal control and self-responsibility.

Self-quieting is what you, or your child, can do to get to a peaceful state of mind where you can work through emotions and find solutions to your problem. Parents need to show children that they don't have to make someone else do something, but can turn within to find solutions and peace.

Create a self-quieting space with your child. This space doesn't have to be your child's bedroom. It could be in the kitchen, the study, a corner tucked away somewhere, or, weather permitting, outside. Help your child find things to bring to her self-quieting space that help her quiet herself and work through her feelings. A tape player with peaceful music, books, play dough, colors, tool bench, or a tree stump with a hammer and nails are possibilities.

Children will learn self-quieting most effectively if you model it for them. For the first few times, you might even go to their self-quieting space with them and show them what to do.

Place three questions on the wall in each self-quieting space:

- What is the problem?
- What is my part in the problem?
- What is one thing I can do to improve the situation?

The following is a list of things to do when you ask your child to take a self-quieting break:

- Get on the child's level, eye to eye, and speak calmly and lovingly.

- Say to him, "It looks like you need a break. Go to your self-quieting place. Come back when you're calm and ready to move on or resolve the problem." Say this once, and only once to your child.

- If your child does not leave, pick him up or lead him gently and lovingly to his self-quieting space.

- If your child comes back and acts appropriately, let him stay. If his behavior is not appropriate, take him back to his space without saying a word. You may have to take him out of the room several times. Be patient and persistent.

When you tell your child, "Come back when you're ready," you're teaching him to act from an internal sense of control. If you say, "Come out in five minutes," you have decided when he's ready.

When my son Tyler was two and a half years old, I had invited some friends over for dinner. At dinner, Tyler started acting inappropriately. I first asked him to stop. He calmed down for a few seconds and then began to misbehave again. I gently picked him up and took him to another room. I said, "You may come back when you're ready." He came back immediately and continued to act inappropriately. I picked him up and took him out of the room. This time I didn't say a thing. He came in again and acted inappropriately. This time his father took him out. We must have taken him out of the room fourteen times. After the fourteenth time, Tyler sat for a whole hour at the table without being inappropriate.

Couples have an advantage when they agree to use the same discipline method because they can take turns with a persistent child. You may think, "Fourteen times! Who has the time to do that?!" Yes, it took patience to do this the first time, but the more I used the method, the more quickly Tyler responded.

You may want to devise a signal or use a special word to give each other when you notice that self-quieting is needed. One family I know uses the peace sign of the '60's. A preschool calls the self-quieting room their "happy place," because the children go there to collect their thoughts and return to the group in a happy frame of mind.

If your child's goal is revenge or power, you may get into a battle with him about taking a self-quieting break. Stop what you're doing and take the self-quieting break yourself.

Setting limits

Limits tell your family under what condition you are willing or unwilling to do something. They signify where you "draw the line." They tell people what you will or will not tolerate. The purpose of limits is to take care of you. Limits are not designed to control or manipulate someone else's behavior.

Mother was playing basketball with her two teenage sons. The boys were getting competitive, and soon the game was no fun. Mother announced, "It's not fun for me when you two fight. When you're ready to make it fun again, come and get me. I'd love to play again."

I was holding hands and roller skating with my daughter. She said in a very demanding tone of voice, "Skate faster!" This wasn't the first time I had noticed she was being demanding, so I said, "I'm unwilling to have you talk like that to me. It makes me feel like not cooperating with you. If you continue, I'll skate by myself."

Nita asked Mom to take her to the video store and rent her a movie. She had already spent her allowance for the week. Mom said, "I'd be willing to take you to the video store, but I'm unwilling to rent you a movie."

Limits give others important information about you to help them know what they can or cannot expect from you. Limits are about your needs, not about criticizing someone else's behavior or about trying to make them act in a certain way.

Why do children need limits?

Children need limits so they can learn to recognize and respect other people's limits. Limits provide a sense of security, as well. Without them, children feel abandoned and confused, and sometimes misbehave in order to find limits. Limits make children feel that we care about them.

Children need limits to learn how to deal with conflict, too. What happens when they disregard someone's limits? What happens when someone disrespects theirs? Children need limits to help them define themselves. Limits help your children set their own as they watch you model asserting yours.

Limits help children learn what is socially acceptable. They need to learn that if they go past a certain point, there will be consequences. Some may be serious, such as getting in trouble with the law.

When are limits needed?

Some common limits you may want to set concern the use of your belongings, radio and television, bedtime, your time, profanity, mealtime, chores, care and feeding of pets, and car. This is not a complete list by any means. Add to it things that are important in your family.

Violations of limits

The best clue to whether or not your limits are violated is how you feel. If you feel any of these emotions, your limits are being dishonored, or you're not clear about them:

angry	abused
resentful	smothered
overburdened	unappreciated
taken advantage of	torn between people you love

Why is it hard to set limits?

Your ability to set limits and follow through is largely determined by how you were parented as a child. Children who had no limits set for them or were unsupervised much of the time grow up not knowing how to set their own limits. Children who suffered put downs like, "Don't make waves," "Children should be seen and not heard," and "You're being selfish" also have trouble setting limits.

Girls, especially, who were told it wasn't proper to assert themselves have a hard time feeling worthy of setting limits. Abuse in homes–mental, physical, emotional, sexual, drugs or alcohol, or work–all violate limits and keep people from learning how to set them. Intimidation and fear also do not allow limit setting.

Limits are difficult to set in situations where there is serious illness or disability. If self-sacrifice was modeled and expected of you, limits are even harder to set and observe. It is almost impossible to reconcile your feelings of being overwhelmed with the expectation that you will care for someone else as long and as much as they need. It doesn't matter if the person doesn't ask self-sacrifice of you, but rather what the expectation was that you grew up with that has conditioned you on a basic level.

Sometimes we don't set limits because we don't feel we deserve them. Or we feel guilty about our own actions, such as working too much or getting divorced.

Parents often don't set limits because they're afraid of conflict. Perhaps the child will get angry and reject the parent or leave. Parents may think that setting a limit won't make any difference. Instead of directly setting limits, sometimes we handle problems by:

- Acting or pretending as if nothing happened (denial)
- Ignoring and hoping the problem will go away
- Talking ourselves out of our feelings
- Making excuses for another person's behavior
- Going over and over the event, trying to make sense of it
- Blaming ourselves or someone else

- Getting even with the other person
- Feeling like we're above having those feelings
- Pretending that we don't care
- Withholding love or communication

What to expect when you begin to set limits

When you first start to set limits, expect that your child's behavior will get worse. Children will test you. They will try everything in their power to get you to go back to the way you used to be. So, make sure your seat belt is fastened—you're off on a wild ride!

Steps for setting limits

1. **Honor your feelings.** Remember feelings are neither right nor wrong. They just are.

2. **Be clear about what you want, and what you're willing to do or not do.**

3. **Tell your family, using an "I" statement.** Do not blame, shame, lay on guilt, exaggerate, or complain. Do this step as soon as possible to prevent becoming unnecessarily resentful.

4. **Be ready to "stick to your guns."** Be consistent and follow through. It is imperative that you do what you say. When you don't, children learn that parents are all talk and no action. The sooner you take action, the sooner your child will recognize his limits.

Dad and his two-year-old son were in a donut shop. The boy was wandering around in front of the doorway. Dad was concerned that his son might hurt himself or become a nuisance to the customers entering. He said, "Michael, come here!" Michael seemed to enjoy his act of defiance, and continued to absorb himself in the commotion around the door. Again Dad demanded, "Michael, come here right now or we're leaving!" Dad finally picked up his son and brought him over to the table. Michael went back to the door when he could wiggle away from Dad's clutches. Dad yelled, "Now,

Michael, I'm not going to tell you again, Michael, get away from that door. . . . If I've told you once, I've told you a thousand times. MICHAEL!"

Dad never did follow through with his promise to leave. Dad's words would have been effective if he had given the situation his full attention. He could have given Michael the choice of staying beside him or leaving the donut shop after his first request was ignored. If the child hadn't come away from the door, Dad should have immediately followed through by picking his child up and leaving the shop. Then Michael would have learned that Dad means what he says. If Dad doesn't want to leave, then he shouldn't give Michael that choice.

Whenever you give a choice that you don't intend to honor, you are threatening your child. When you do not follow through, your child will test you. It will become more and more difficult to establish limits. Think carefully (if quickly!) before you set a limit to be sure you can follow through and enforce it when your child tests it. Remember, it is normal for children to test limits.

Consequences

Two types of "consequences" are useful in disciplining children. One is called a natural consequence, in which the result of the child's action is whatever will happen naturally, without any interference from anyone. The other is a logical consequence, in which the response to the child's action derives from something the parent causes to happen.

Use of natural consequences

Ask yourself, "What would happen if I didn't do anything?" That result is a natural consequence. If you take action when you don't need to, you rob your child of the chance to experience the natural consequences of his actions. Natural consequences are very effective teachers.

You can eliminate friction by letting natural consequences take their course because you don't have to nag and remind. The situation itself disciplines your child.

Mother recognized that her twelve-year-old Jenny had developed a habit of forgetting things. Luckily, Mother had heard the expression, "A child who always forgets has a parent who always remembers."

One afternoon, Jenny was making a skirt for a home economics class. She was adding the final touches at home and was supposed to take the skirt to school the next morning. However, Jenny was in a hurry leaving for school the following day and forgot to take the skirt with her. Mother noticed that Jenny had forgotten and resisted the temptation to remind her. Instead, she let natural consequences take effect.

Later that day, Mother received a phone call from Jenny asking her to bring the skirt to school. Mother told her, in a very friendly voice, "No, Jenny, I'm unwilling to do that," and changed the subject.

Jenny got a lesson in remembering out of this experience. Mother would have ruined the learning experience if she had brought the skirt to Jenny or had said, "See what happens when you forget?" Then Jenny could have focused on Mother's critical comment rather than on her own responsibility for remembering.

Natural consequences are more effective than logical consequences, in which you set up the disciplinary action. However, there are three situations when you would want to use a logical consequence instead of a natural one. They are:

- When the natural consequence would be hazardous to the well-being of your child. For example, a natural consequence of playing in the street is she would be hit by a car.

- When the natural consequence interferes with your rights or the rights of others, such as when a teen continues to play music at a loud volume even after he has been asked to turn it down.

- When the effects of the natural consequence are too long

range for the child to connect cause and effect. For example, the natural consequence for a child who does not brush his teeth is cavities.

Use of logical consequences

If self-quieting, setting limits, and natural consequences have not been effective disciplinary tools to solve a particular problem, you may need to use a logical consequence. Your child must recognize the logic of the discipline in order for it to be effective. It's a very common mistake for parents to connect a misdeed to a consequence that has no relevance whatsoever. For example, taking away television privileges for breaking a window is not relevant to the offense. Your child is more likely to believe she's being punished, and rebel. On the other hand, it would be logical for a child to do chores (such as mow lawns) to help pay for the new window pane. Your child is not being punished, but is instead learning to repair his mistake.

For logical consequences to be effective, they must incorporate the following "3 R's of logical consequences." These are: respectful, reasonable, and related.

Respectful

Always show respect for your child. Allow him as much input as possible into the determination of the consequence. Avoid anything that causes your child to feel guilt or shame so that he doesn't view the consequence as a punishment.

Reasonable

Consequences that are excessive or harsh cause your child to focus on what he perceives as punishment, instead of repairing his mistake. He's likely to react in a revengeful way.

Related

The consequence needs to be related to your child's mistake. If he makes a mess, he cleans it up. If he hurts someone, he tries to ease the pain. If he damages something, he repairs or replaces it. Remember that punishment results in anger and resentment, while logical consequences teach him to be responsible for his mistakes.

Logical consequences relate to future behavior

Logical consequences are set up to improve future behavior, not to punish past behavior. If you are in the middle of a conflict, don't try to develop logical consequences at that time. All you'll be able to think of is a "logical punishment" because you're probably upset. Instead, step out of the conflict and take time to calm down. Then, during a peaceful time, take out the logical consequences worksheet on the next page and go through the steps with your child.

Notice that this process is the same as the "Steps for Conflict Resolution" (see pages 71-72), except steps one and seven. The reason for thinking of three things you love about your child is because you're probably feeling angry with your child. It's extremely difficult to think of enjoyable, creative solutions when you're angry. The purpose of step one is to change your attitude so that you will think of a consequence instead of a punishment.

LOGICAL CONSEQUENCES WORKSHEET

1. List three things you love about your child.

   ....

   ....

   ....

2. Ask your child's permission for a particular time to work out a logical consequence together.

3. Write, "I want . . . " Say what you want to have happen and why, simply and clearly, without guilt, blame, shame, and exaggerations.

   ....

4. Ask your child what he or she wants and why. Write that down, too.

   ....

   ....

5. Brainstorm a list of possible solutions with your child on a separate sheet of paper.

6. Create a solution to the problem from the list. Let your child cross off unacceptable solutions first, then you do the same. Choose one suggestion or a combination of suggestions you both like and write it down.

   ....

   ....

7. Acknowledge your child for cooperating. Say, "Thanks for working this out with me. What should I do if you happen to forget?" Now come up with a logical consequence using either your child's suggestion, which works best, or your suggestion. Once you have discussed and agreed on a logical consequence, write it down.

   ....

   ....

8. After you have used the logical consequence for a certain time, ask yourself, "Did I get results that were good for my child and me? Do I need to improve the logical consequence?" You can start the process all over again, if necessary. Sometimes you need to try more than one solution.

Dad bought his two boys new bicycles, helmets, and locks. Neither boy seemed able to get in the habit of locking up his bike, in spite of punishment, rewards, bribes, and threats from the parents, who were at their wits' end.

Dad decided to try a logical consequence, instead. He told the boys (when he was feeling calm and friendly), "There's a situation I'd like to change. Is this a good time to talk?" "Yeah," said the boys. Dad continued, "I've noticed I've been bugging you guys about locking your bikes. That makes you mad, doesn't it?" The boys looked puzzled and answered with some hesitation, "Yeah . . ."

Dad went on, "I think I've figured out why I have a problem. I realize I gave you the bikes and they're yours. It's really not my business if you choose to risk having them stolen. However, I would feel bad. They were expensive, and I'm not willing to buy two more bikes. Do you guys have any ideas about how I can solve my problem?"

The boys told Dad they would lock up the bikes. Dad said, "Thanks, that would solve the problem. What should I do if you forget?" Both boys replied, "I don't know." "Well, how about I lock them up if you forget?" asked Dad. "Okay," said the boys. "We'll try that for a few weeks and see how it works. If you boys think of a better idea, we'll talk about it," said their dad.

A few mornings later, Tom came running into the house shouting, "Somebody chained our bikes to the porch!" His mom resisted the temptation to explain and, instead, simply smiled and gave him a pat on the shoulder. Five minutes later, Tom came back inside, saying, "I locked my bike with my lock now. Would you take the chain off?" Mom replied in a friendly tone, "Dad has the key and he's at work." Tom asked, "Will you drive us to school?" Mom said lovingly, "Sorry, that would make me late to work." Tom and his brother had to walk to school that morning.

When Dad came home and found both boys had locked their bikes, he removed the chain. About two weeks later, the boys forgot again, and Dad chained the bikes to the porch. From that day on, the boys remembered to lock their bikes.

Logical consequences can also be set without using steps 5 and 6 on the previous page (Logical Consequences Worksheet).

Mom called, "Sue, do you have a minute?" "Sure, Mom," said Sue.

"I have something I'd like to change. I've been yelling at you a lot lately and I bet that makes you feel bad," said Mom. Sue answered, "Yeah." Mom continued, "The reason I'm yelling is that some days you decide not to take out the garbage and I feel like I have to do all the work. What do you think I could do about my problem?" Sue mumbled, "I don't know."

Mom said, "Well, how about I try this. I don't want to be telling you what to do. You can choose to take the garbage out or not. If by 4 p.m. you haven't taken it out, then I'll do it instead of driving you to soccer practice. In other words, I'm willing to be the chauffeur or the garbage person, but not both. Is that okay with you?" Sue answered, "Oh, Mom, I'll take the garbage out." Mom said, "Thanks a lot, that will help me. What should I do if some morning you forget? We all forget sometimes." Sue said, "Nothing." "I'm unwilling to do nothing. How about we try what I've suggested? If you think of a different plan, let me know and we'll see what we can work out," answered Mom.

If you create a logical consequence and discover that it isn't working, and maybe the problem has worsened, then perhaps you really are using punishment.

My experience shows that the most effective consequences have outcomes the child actually enjoys. This is especially true with children who have the goals of revenge or power.

What children may say

Parents can increase the likelihood of working out effective logical consequences when they know how to handle kids' responses to the process. Children may say, "I don't know" when asked for ideas. You can say, "Then how about we try this . . . and if you think of a different plan, let me know. We'll see what we can work out." Some children may want a solution you don't like. Is so, say, "I'm unwilling to do that. Do you have another suggestion?"

If your child has been accustomed to punishment, he may say, "If I don't clean my room, you can spank me." You're trying a new way to discipline, so you may say, "I'm unwilling to hurt you. What else do you suggest?" Don't be fooled into thinking that if he selects a punishment, that makes it okay.

If your child suggests a reasonable consequence and you agree to it, say, "I'll try that for a week. Thanks." If he declares that he will not repeat the offense, or mistake, and he's not good at keeping his word, say, "Thanks. That will make things better for me. What would you like me to do if you break this agreement?"

By the way, if you just read the Worksheet without filling it in, you should know that change is much more likely when you take the time think through and write down what you decide to do.

Mini-logical consequences

It is sometimes expedient for a parent to apply a logical consequence without going through the planning process and using a worksheet. When you, the parent alone, apply a mini-logical consequence, you do something that is logically related to your child's behavior. For example, if your child spills his milk, you hand him a dishrag.

Mom was continually nagging her two children to unroll their dirty socks before they put them in the clothes hamper. She decided to try a mini-logical consequence. She simply didn't wash socks that were rolled up. After two weeks, all the rolled up socks were still in the hamper and Mom said nothing. A few days later she noticed that all the socks were still in the hamper, but someone had unrolled them. From that day on, both kids were more diligent about unrolling their socks, and a word had never been spoken. The family atmosphere had not been disturbed and the kids didn't feel bossed around. They cooperated.

Summary of consequences

Natural consequences

A natural consequence flows out of events. The parent does not do anything to interfere, arrange, or impose.

Logical consequences

Parent and child meet together to decide upon a mutually agreeable solution to a problem. The consequence is logically related to the child's behavior. Logical consequences are used when a good relationship exists between parent and child.

Mini-logical consequences

Parent makes an impromptu decision without discussing with the child, The consequence is logically related to the child's behavior and is applied.

Results of discipline

To make sure you are on target with discipline and your child is learning what you wish her to learn, ask yourself these questions:

- What happens to your child after she's disciplined? Is she angry? Do you see her trying to get back at you in an underhanded way? Is she fully cooperating or is she withdrawn and sullen?

- What happens to her self-esteem? Is it lowered or enhanced?

- Does she feel empowered to repair her mistake?

- Does she become more externally motivated or internally motivated?

- What happens to your relationship? Is communication better? Because of your discipline, will she be more or less likely to tell you about her mistakes in the future? Will she be too afraid? Did you win the battle (get the child to do what you wanted) and lose the war (dampen your delicate relationship)?

- Does the interaction encourage your child to discuss her wants and feelings? Or does she become hesitant to express her feelings or opinions?

- Does the interaction improve her ability to solve conflicts in a way that allows both of you to win?

- Does she learn about her behavior in a way that provides increased choices? Or does she learn that she has no choice at all?

8

Siblings: War or Peace?

no activity provokes more frustration and anger in parents than sibling fights. Parents try many ways to stop them, but without apparent success. Sometimes, you can stop the fight that's in progress, but nothing you do seems effective in preventing the fights that will start tomorrow. Parents often tolerate and accept fighting as inevitable. With all the other problems in our lives, sibling fights don't get the problem-solving attention they deserve. However, when you look globally at what happens when people fight over possessions, territory, philosophies, resources, and race, you see war. We need to practice a new way of being that creates peace, and the place to start is in our families.

It may seem a bit extreme to compare our children's fights to war. However, our children are the future leaders of the world. Wouldn't it be great if they learned win/win negotiation skills in childhood, and then could bring these skills into our governments?

Parents have a tremendous opportunity to contribute to peace by dealing with children's fights so that children learn to solve their differences in a peaceful manner. We need to encourage values of peacefulness and cooperation. World peace begins in the hearts and homes of our families. When the consciousness changes in our homes, it will change in our governments and in our world community, as well.

Techniques to help prevent problems

Children can learn a number of nonviolent ways to prevent problems. Home is a good place to begin learning and practicing these skills with your help.

Demonstrate self-control and relaxation

A good place to start learning peaceful ways to solve problems is to take care of the mental and physical response to anger. Teach your child to breathe deeply in through his nose and out through his mouth to the count of ten when he feels angry. This will relax him and give him time to think before acting. Model using this technique yourself and, at the same time, express your emotions clearly and calmly.

Encourage assertiveness

Some children are taken advantage of because they don't stand up for themselves; then they become angry. Teach your unassertive child to yell, "Stop it!" in an ever louder voice (this may be hard for her to do at first), until the offender backs off. Another technique is for your child to hold out her hand and say, "This is my space," in a loud voice. Unassertive children often use quiet, whiny voices, so you may have to help your child practice using a strong voice.

Show how to take turns and trade

Many problems among siblings arise when both want to use the same toy, or ball, or clothes, or whatever (depending on their ages). Teach children how to take turns or to trade one thing for another. It helps to use an impartial aid like a timer to let a child know how long she has to wait before she gets a turn and how long the other child gets to play with or use the object.

Teach children how to care

Teach your children to consider each other's feelings. Any solution to a problem they decide on needs to take feelings into account. You could say, "Eric looks sad. What could you do or say to help him feel better?"

Model respect and joy in play

Children need to learn how to join others in play in ways that are positive. Aggressive or whiny children are not welcome playmates. You can role play with dolls or puppets with a child who is having trouble learning how to play with others. Let him or her play with two creatures, and you be the third who wants to join the fun. Behave in ways that are not acceptable and talk about what to do differently. Then play that way so your child can practice.

Describe what you see and empathize

Describe without judgment what you see occurring during the children's fight. When you bring to their conscious awareness what they're doing, they then can choose if they want to continue. If you speak judgmentally, the children are likely to become defensive.

Concentrate on win/win negotiation

Teach children to negotiate a solution to their differences. A negotiation means that both kids get what they want and need, though this may be different at the end of the negotiation than what they thought it to be when they began. Negotiation is different from compromise, in which neither child is satisfied and may be more concerned with what he gave up than what he got.

Children can't negotiate in the heat of anger. If they are angry, or become angry again, stop negotiating and go back to describing their differences and empathizing with them until they calm down.

Teamwork and cooperation are essential tools of negotiation. Say, "Let's see what we can do by working together. How good are you guys at teamwork?" You want to minimize competition, so avoid saying, "Let's see who can do this first." Noncompetitive games can help children get used to the idea of both winning.

Put children in the same boat

[Crash!]

Mother rushed downstairs to find her favorite lamp in pieces on the floor. "All right, who did this?" she demanded of her two children.

"Mike did it," volunteered Sarah, pointing her finger accusingly at him. "I did not, you liar. You did it," screamed Mike. "You both know how I hate it when you lie. Now, tell me, which one of you broke the lamp?" demanded Mother. Neither would own up to the deed. Finally, Mother turned to Mike and said, "You always seem to get into trouble and you're the oldest. You should know better. Now, you clean up the mess, and no TV for you the rest of the week, young man!"

This mother has given her children negative information rather than positive skills. She needs to go back upstairs and come down with a fresh viewpoint.

[Crash!]

Mother rushed downstairs to find her favorite lamp in pieces on the floor. She felt very angry, so she stopped and took ten deep breaths until she calmed down. She said to the children, "It looks like you two had an accident."

Before she could say anything more, both kids began to accuse the other. Mother put her arms around both of them and said, "I'm sad my lamp is broken. It doesn't matter who broke it. I wonder if you two would like some help cleaning up the pieces?"

After the three of them cleaned up the mess, Mom said, "Would the two of you be willing to contribute fifty cents a week from now until Christmas to help pay for the lamp?" "But, Mom, that's not fair! I didn't break it," wailed Sarah. "Do you have a better idea?" Mother asked. "Yeah, make Mike pay for it. He broke it," Sarah said. Mother responded, "I'm not willing to do that. I don't want to take sides. If you have any other suggestions, let me know. In the meantime, I'll deduct fifty cents from both of your allowances."

You might be saying right now that the mother's action isn't fair to both children. There is no way to be fair; there is a way to be effective. She chose to put the children in the same boat and hold them both responsible for the accident. Neither child was made to feel special, either for being good or being bad. The child who is the troublemaker often changes his or her behavior when he or she no longer gets special attention for it. Furthermore, this mother modeled handling anger in a clear and calm manner.

I was driving the camp van when two campers began to argue. I didn't say a word, but looked for a safe place to pull the van over. I stopped, got out, and sat down on the hillside. One of the kids came to me and asked, "What's wrong?" I said, "It's discouraging to listen to arguing, so I'm waiting until you're finished." The boy ran back to the van and reported to the others. Soon all the boys called out, "Come on back. We solved the argument." I got back in the van and we continued. On the way back to camp, another argument erupted. As soon as I began to slow down, the boys stopped fighting.

Sometimes it is neither safe nor convenient to stop the car when children fight. In that case, you may have to do something different. One dad told his children that he would turn around and go home if they didn't stop arguing by the time he reached the stoplight. They didn't stop, so he kept his word and turned around. If you want kids to learn, follow through instead of making idle threats.

Set the stage for peace in your family

You need to set the stage for peaceful interaction before you can teach the kids how to solve differences. Sometimes nothing more is needed. There are at least six important things you can do.

Stay out of the fight

Sometimes a parent's best response to a fight is to stay out of it. This is particularly true if the children are fighting to get your attention. You will need to teach them how to get your attention more appropriately, but for now you want to remove yourself from their vicinity so that they will quit fighting.

If you're worried that the children might damage something in the house, firmly and gently guide them outside. If you think they might hurt each other, remain silently vigilant in an out-of-the-way spot. Remove any weapons (sticks, toys, etc.) from their hands silently and gently.

Leave the area or the house altogether if the kids are old enough. Don't say anything as you go, because you don't want them to feel guilty, nor do you want them to feel that they have power over you.

My sister and I used to fight when we were children. Our parents tried lots of ideas to get us to stop, including putting us in the corner or making us kiss ("Yuck!") and make up. Even though we stopped fighting for the moment, we were still angry with each other. One day, during a fight, my mother left the house without saying a word. When we realized she was gone, we thought about how uncomfortable our fighting was for us and how inconsiderate we were of her. We quit fighting, and we cleaned up the kitchen. We wanted to surprise her, and make amends for discouraging her.

Mother's departure made more of an impact on us than punishment ever did. She left the choice to stop fighting up to us. While she was gone, we worked together, which brought us closer.

Act in an unexpected way

Sometimes it's possible to dispel tension or a fight by doing something unexpected. For example, if your children are calling each other names, join in playfully. If they are starting to roughhouse too angrily, propose a walk or a game of ball together.

Josh angrily yelled at Andrea, "You're a stupid cow!" Andrea yelled back, "Well, you're a stupid monkey breath." Dad heard this exchange and after observing for a few seconds, said lightly, "This is a great game," and turned to Josh, "You're a slimy, green piece of mildewed spaghetti left over in the refrigerator!" Then he beckoned to Andrea and said, "Your turn." They continued as everyone took turns. Minutes later they were all laughing about how creative and funny they were.

Eliminate tattling

Children tattle to get others in trouble, to get attention, or to get you to solve their problem. If you tell them to solve their problem themselves, or teach them to get attention appropriately, they will usually quit tattling. If your child says, "Mom, Jared hit me!" say, "That must hurt. I wonder how you'll handle that?"

Deal with jealousy and anger

It seems impossible to keep children from feeling jealous of one another because we can never control how they're going to interpret what they hear and see. You can correct them when they think you favor one over the other and you can minimize the discomfort of jealousy, however. Teach your child that she is whole and complete in herself without being the same as her sibling.

Jennifer complained to Mom, "I'm not as smart as Nathan." Mom said, "It's not important that you be the same. I love the fact that you are different from Nathan. Both of you are smart in your own, different ways. Why would I want two Nathans? Besides, if you decide to enjoy learning, you'll be amazed at what you can do."

Be careful not to compare her to her sibling; be careful that you do not favor one child over another. Parents who try to make everything fair for each child fight a losing battle, and give both children the wrong message that they are the same and should always have the same things. Children whose parents honor and nurture their individual differences feel less competitive toward other children, even if they are jealous at times.

Siblings get angry with one another when they are:

- Forced to share toys, clothes, equipment, space, etc. Be sure your child has some things he doesn't have to share.

- Feel like their needs take second place to their siblings'. Be sure to meet each child's needs in an appropriate manner. This can be hard if one sibling is very ill, for example. Just do the best you can.

- Told they should not be angry with one another. This is the way parents teach their children to stuff their feelings. The feelings don't go away; they go underground and are likely to intensify because they're never dealt with in a healthy way. Empathize with your child's anger; let him say he's angry out-loud. If he says, "I hate my brother!" you can say, "I can understand that you're really angry with Jason right now." Teach your son conflict resolution skills.

Bring peace to the fight

You need your children's attention in order to teach them new skills. If you have dealt with the issues above and the kids are still fighting, move on to creating a more peaceful atmosphere so that they can learn.

Sit or stoop down to the children's level when they're smaller than you are. Touch them lovingly, perhaps by rubbing their backs. Look at each of them with acceptance, without judgment or anger. If they're fighting over a toy, wait until they get calm and then hold out your hand for the object that they're fighting over. After they give you the object, tell them, "You may have the toy back when the two of you have come to agreement about it." Then leave the room with the toy and let them work out their problem if they have the skills. Don't use intimidation to get them to stop fighting. Avoid saying, "You're driving me crazy with your fighting!" or, "If you don't stop fighting, I'm going to lock you in your rooms!"

Jenny and Andrea are fighting over a shirt, and it's the kind of fight they have often. Mother has decided to do something different this time. Let's see how it goes:

Jenny yells, "Give that shirt back to me!"

Andrea screams as she hits, "No, I had it first!"

Jenny hits back, "Quit hitting me! You're ripping my shirt!"

Mom gets down on their level, strokes them lovingly on their backs, and describes, "It looks like you two are really angry with each other!"

Andrea, calming slightly, says: "Mom, Jenny took my shirt again without asking."

Mom empathizes, "It's difficult to share clothes with one another."

Jenny replies, "Yeah, she won't let me wear her shirt."

Andrea retorts, "Well, you never ask me. You just take it and then you don't wash it. Then it's dirty when I want to wear it."

At this point, the girls are calm enough to pay attention when their mother starts to teach them conflict resolution skills. Watch how careful she is to be nonjudgmental, to listen to both of them without taking sides, and to let them reach a solution themselves.

Mom asks, "Well, Andrea, how could you both win? What do you think that Jenny wants?"

Andrea says, "She wants me to ask when I want to wear her shirt and she wants me to wash it when I'm through."

Mom asks, "Is that accurate, Jenny?"

Jenny says, "Yeah, she never asks!"

Mom suggests, "So, if Andrea asks before she takes your shirt and she washes it when she's done, then you both will win?"

Jenny replies, "Yeah, that's right."

Mom suggests, "Ask Andrea for exactly what you want. Say, 'What I want is . . .'

Jenny repeats, "What I want is for you to ask before you take my shirt, and I want you to wash it when you're done."

Andrea answers, "Okay, I'd be willing to do that."

Mom says, "Thanks for working that out. I think it's great that you're willing to share your clothes with each other."

The two girls have learned more by Mom doing a little coaching than if she had yelled at them, or solved the problem herself.

Deal with sibling competition

Sibling competition does not necessarily mean one child beats up on the other. Another way to compete is for one child to give up in an area where his sibling succeeds in order to avoid comparison. One child might excel in music and the other in sports. Often, the child who doesn't do well in the area of his sibling's expertise feels that he doesn't have talent in that area. In reality, he has only given up. With practice, he too could achieve in that area, if he chooses.

Children can compete in other subtle ways. You may have a "good" child and a "bad" child. Listen to this woman's admission:

I have to confess that in my family, I was the "good" girl and I had a brother who was always getting punished. One day, we were in back of the garage where there was a sledge hammer. I looked at my brother and said, "Boy, that sure looks heavy, doesn't it?" He said, "Yeah, it sure does." Tauntingly, I said, "I bet it would really hurt if someone got hit with it." He got a big grin on his face and leaned over to pick up the hammer. I said, "If you hit me with that, I'm telling!" He picked it up and tapped me on the shoulder. I ran into the house screaming, "Mommy, Andy hit me with a sledge hammer!" Mother held me until I quieted down, and then she lectured and spanked Andy. I felt pretty smug about the whole thing.

You can see that sometimes the younger sibling is not the poor innocent victim she pretends to be. If you have a "good" child and a "bad" child, and you decide to work on the "bad" child's behavior, be prepared for some surprises. When your parenting becomes effective at changing the bad child's behavior, your "good" child may start to misbehave. Believe it or not, this is a sign of progress. Pat yourself on the back because it means you have succeeded in making the behavior of both children inappropriate. You have disturbed the equilibrium.

9

Putting It All Together

Thise are the steps to redirecting children's behavior that you have learned
in reading this book. The material is
gathered here in brief form to help you
remember the new philosophy and the
skills that enable you to redirect children's
behavior for the benefit of everyone in your
family.

1. **Establish and maintain a relationship of acceptance and mutual
   respect with your child.** Make a loving connection with eye contact,
   touch, and an accepting tone of voice.
   Encourage your child to express his or
   her own opinions and feelings.

2. **Gain insight into your child's mistaken goal.** You can determine his or her goal by the way the child's behavior makes you feel. Refer to Chapter 6.

3. **Help your child identify his or her mistaken goal** in a nonaccusing way.

Children are often unaware of what they're doing. This step brings his or her goal to consciousness, and gives the child the opportunity to make a different choice.

Speak in neutral terms, like, "It feels like you'd like some attention," instead of, "You have been really stubborn lately." Other phrases that work are, "Could it be that you want to have a power struggle about this?" or, "I'm wondering if you want to be left alone?" or, "That hurts. Are you wanting to hurt me?" It is vital that your intention be one of understanding and curiosity, and not to get information to manipulate or control your child.

If you are unable, for whatever reason, to speak in a nonaccusing way, skip step 3 because you will only set up a power struggle.

4. **Arrange or allow a situation that makes your child's goal inappropriate.** Techniques that you can use to make a child's behavior inappropriate are natural and logical consequences, doing the unexpected, and using signals.

5. **Redirect behavior** by providing opportunities for your child to:
   - Be powerful in appropriate ways
   - Be helpful, and recognize the value of feeling worthwhile
   - Be cooperative, and recognize how much more can be achieved by working as a team
   - Be a participant, and recognize the variety and fun that comes from being involved
   - Do what he can to make the situation more enjoyable

- Learn that problems don't need to be "fixed," but only improved.

This step is essential because, if you just stop their misbehavior, children will misbehave again since you have only worked on the symptom and not the cause of the behavior. Positive action gives the child somewhere to rechannel that negative energy.

Our children, our future

The way we parent will, to a large extent, determine the future of our society. We have a choice: to parent in a way that teaches our children to be uncooperative, self-serving, irresponsible, and unconnected, or to raise children who hold values deeply, are compassionate, and maintain and nurture close relationships. The choice is ours.

I do not intend to make you feel guilty–as we know, guilt serves no one. My intention, instead, is to increase your awareness of how your actions affect our entire society. I strongly urge that you become more conscious. Don't settle for less than you can do! Set goals for the way you want your family to be, and then consciously create the family of your heart's deepest desire. You and your family are extremely capable and creative. The fact that you are reading this book tells me of your concern, and I applaud and appreciate your commitment.

It is no easy task to change old patterns. Make sure you are gentle with yourself. Find someone to support you–perhaps a spouse, a friend, or a parenting class. Without support, it's all too easy to slip back into old, less positive ways.

Most important of all, love one another and be good to one another. The individual members of your family can function like a battery, that is, a collective, recharging source of encouragement and support that allows all of you to go out into the community and do the things you need to do. There is nothing more important than loving someone and being loved. Remember this.

A Child's Request

Dear Mommy and Daddy,

Hold me, touch me, snuggle me often, for it is through your love that I flourish.

Watch me, listen to me, take your time with me when you read *Green Eggs and Ham* to me at night, for I judge my importance by how important I am to you.

Be patient, understand me first, whenever possible help me to get what I want, for it is through your interactions that I learn to interact with others.

Don't be afraid to be firm with me, for it is through your firmness that I learn the courage to care.

Don't bribe me, reward me, or punish me, for you rob me of the opportunity to listen to my own internal voice.

Don't hit me or yell at me, for this teaches me to use force to get my way.

Forgive yourself quickly, for my spirit is resilient.

Instead of remembering my footprints on your windshield, my impish protests, and the hole I put in the wall, remember the day I discovered my shadow, my arms around your neck, and the delight of my giggles.

I will remember your butterfly kisses, your open arms, dancing in the rain with you, and the plastic frog you put under my eggs at breakfast more than the toys and clothes you bought for me.

On our bad days, watch me while I sleep. Marvel at my eyelashes, cheekbones, and fingertips, and remind yourself of how much you love me.

When given a choice, assume the best of me and expect the best for me.

Stand by me, but let me fight my own battles, for it is here that I develop my own strength and build my own character.

Support my ever-changing dreams. I need someone to believe in me when I don't.

Trust me as a teen, even though there is no evidence that you should. Trust that you have taught me well.

Allow me to express who I am and make my life's decisions, even though they differ from yours.

Lastly, make nothing other than God more important than our family, for it is here that I discover who I am.

–Kathryn J. Kvols

Appendix

Common Behaviors: Ages 18 Months to 18 Years

What follows is a brief summary of the normal behaviors of children at different ages. Sometimes when you understand why your child is doing what he's doing, it's easier to muster up the patience to deal with the behavior. Also, many parents worry if their child is normal. Biting and hitting are behaviors of concern to parents of two-year-olds. This behavior is quite normal for a toddler. Knowing this fact lets a parent breathe a sigh of relief. However, just because the behavior is normal at this stage does not mean that it goes undisciplined. Parents need to know that they will have to do more educating and disciplining during their child's early years. This is also very normal.

The Gesell Institute for Human Development suggest that easy ages tend to alternate with difficult ages. Ages of equilibrium—inward looking, quiet, withdrawn—tend to be followed by ages of disequilibrium—outward looking, exuberant, expansive. Easier times are followed by more difficult times. A break-up of a calmer period usually is followed by a more mature stage of development.

Don't get concerned if your child is ahead or behind these stages, or if the descriptions don't even resemble what your child does. Every child is an individual. One child may exhibit some of these behaviors while a sibling from the same family may not.

There are many delightful qualities during each age that far outweigh the negatives, or challenges, you see here. However, this book concentrates on how to redirect misbehavior, so the information here is particularly helpful in that regard.

Read the stage before and after your child's age for more information that may be relevant to your situation.

18 Months

Possible annoying, normal behaviors

Is negative, says "No" often.

Does the opposite of what is requested.

Does not want to share; everything is "my" or "mine."

Often hits, kicks, and bites.

Lacks patience, wants it now.

Tests limits (can be quite exhausting).

May climb out of crib.

Refuses to eat certain foods.

Regresses to baby food or bottle.

Clings anxiously or walks away from parent.

Hates to see doors closed.

Is afraid of strangers, including grandparents.

Notices and overreacts to small differences.

Resists diaper change.

Sucks thumb; requires "blankie."

Fears tubs and baths.

Explores genitalia.

Tries to walk away from parent whenever possible.

Does not play with other children; plays alongside or alone.

Does not sit very long for cuddling; stiffens and slides off lap.

2-Year-Olds

Possible annoying, normal behaviors

Has difficulty making decisions; changes her mind even when you
know she wants what is being offered.

Throws temper tantrums, which can be violent.

Demands that things remain the same.

May favor one parent over the other.

Is bossy and demanding.

May start to stutter.

Thumb sucking may intensify.

Dawdles.

Shifts from being capable, "Me do it," to incapable, "Mommy do
it" quickly.

Is easily frustrated.

Does not like to be physically restricted.

Is not interested in pleasing you.

3-Year-Olds

Possible annoying, normal behaviors

Hands may tremble.

Is confused about which hand to use.

Stutters.

May complain about problems with vision.

Seems like nothing pleases him.

Makes commands like, "Don't look at me," "Don't talk."

Is emotionally inconsistent, one minute shy, next minute too bold.

Indulges in nail biting, thumb sucking, picking his nose, and rubbing his genitals.

Expresses fears.

May be cooperative with a baby sitter and a monster for you.

May quit napping.

May still wet the bed.

4-Year-Olds

Possible annoying, normal behaviors

Talks too much.

Incessantly asks, "Why?"

Is fascinated with bowel movements.

Uses words related to elimination, like "poopoo head."

Swears and cusses.

Her demands can be annoyingly persistent.

Excludes certain children from her play.

Wants to know exact details on difficult subjects.

5-Year-Olds

Possible annoying, normal behaviors

Tends to be brash, combative, indecisive, overdemanding, and explosive.

Becomes more challenging in his rebellion, "Try and make me!" is a typical stance.

Once an emotional outburst has started, he may have a hard time stopping it.

Has difficulty grasping a pencil and may change grasps frequently.

Talks too much.

Has difficulty admitting that he has done anything wrong.

May take things that don't belong to him.

Talks with his mouth full.

He can dress himself, but frequently refuses or says, "I can't."

May still suck thumb, pick nose, bite nails.

May clear throat frequently and make clicking or smacking noises.

May be fascinated by fire; may want to start fires.

6-Year-Olds

Possible annoying, normal behaviors

Is extremely ambivalent; can't make up her mind.

Reverses numbers and letters.

Wants to be the first, the best, the winner.

Failure is unbearable.

Has difficulty accepting criticism.

Is loud and demanding.

Acts "fresh."

Is very sensitive emotionally.

Doesn't always tell the truth.

Frequently steals.

Has bad table manners.

May have an occasional toileting accident.

May refuse to bathe.

Battles over dressing.

Doesn't take care of clothes.

Scalp is very tender and sensitive.

Makes irritating, throaty noises.

Is clumsy.

Complains of aches and pains.

7-Year-Olds

Possible annoying, normal behaviors

May be afraid that others don't like him.

Worries.

Minor illness may be magnified to fatality status.

Accuses parents of liking other siblings more.

Is easily disappointed.

Has a tendency to do one thing too long.

Is too anxious to be perfect.

Complains about how others treat her (teachers, siblings, friends).

Has many fears.

Is easily distracted at mealtime.

8-Year-Olds

Possible annoying, normal behaviors

Does everything fast.

Feels extremely sensitive to perceived criticism from others.

Experiences self-doubt.

Hard on himself for making mistakes.

Exaggerates his problems and dilemmas.

Wants a lot of communication with his primary caretaker.

Frequently asks, "What?"

Highly aware of others' mistakes and points them out.

Is not a good self-starter.

Loves to argue.

Wants to wear "what other kids are wearing."

Is accident prone.

May refuse to take baths.

Has strong interest in possessions. May hoard or gloat over them.

9-Year-Olds

Possible annoying, normal behaviors

May now seem to resent her parents' presence.

Wants more freedom.

Wants much social activity.

Has mood swings.

Worries and complains.

Is so busy with her own activity that she seems unaware of others.

Wants fairness.

Bathing can still be a problem.

Lays much blame and emphasis on who started what.

10-Year-Olds

Possible annoying, normal behaviors

Anger is often violent.

Plots revenge.

Has difficulty taking a joke on himself.

Asks personal questions.

May express concern if he isn't developing physically like others.

A girl will hunch her shoulders if she's uncomfortable about breast development.

11-Year-Olds

Possible annoying, normal behaviors

Makes no effort to cooperate.

Is quick to criticize.

Expects perfection from others.

Challenges rules and restrictions.

Loves to argue.

Is physically violent. May hit, kick, or slam doors.

Yells, swears, talks back, says mean and sarcastic things.

Likes to gossip.

Has intense need to be right or to know it all.

Makes references to your "old age."

Needs sleep.

Has difficulty with siblings close in age.

Wants radio or television on while doing homework.

Is always on the phone.

May cheat.

May steal with peers.

Has mood swings.

12-Year-Olds

Possible annoying, normal behaviors

Doing things on weekends with friends is crucial. If he can't, he
may become sullen and depressed.

Expresses boredom if friends are unavailable.

May not want you to purchase clothes for him anymore.

May walk ahead of you or behind you.

May not want to be touched in public.

13-Year-Olds

Possible annoying, normal behaviors

Is uncommunicative.

Withdraws to room frequently.

Demands more privacy and accuses you of prying.

Is uncertain about herself and life in general.

May be unfriendly and unhappy.

Worries about body features.

Does not want to be understood.

Has fewer friends.

Speaks in a low voice.

Shrugs her shoulders.

Feels teachers are unjust.

May be found crying in her room.

Worries about everything.

Expressions of affection don't come easily.

Doesn't often confide in parents.

Is embarrassed by parents.

14-Year-Olds

Possible annoying, normal behaviors

In public, he wants to be as far away from you as possible.

Picks at the way you dress or look.

Revolts at your old-fashioned ways.

Picks apart social systems: school, church, law enforcement, etc.

May challenge cherished family values.

15-Year-Olds

Possible annoying, normal behaviors

Wants to be totally independent and free.

Angry at parents who don't see her as ready for independence.

Age where the family is most unsatisfactory.

Age where friends mean the most.

Has difficulty getting along with the same sex parent.

Does things which cause you great anxiety.

Withdraws all emotional contact with parent.

16- to 18-Year-Olds

Possible annoying, normal behaviors

Teens experience much anxiety about wanting to leave home and doubting their ability to make it.

Feel anxious about what they're going to choose for a career.

May make life unbearable for you.

Other Interesting Books

Children: The Challenge by Rudolf Dreikurs, M.D. New York: Penguin USA, 1991.

Common Ground Handbook for Parents and Teens by Ruth Angran, M.Ed., Patricia Bacus, Kathryn Kvols, Myrna Neims, Ph.D. and Ruth Smith. Gainesville, Florida: Banks Communication, 1996.

Essence of Parenting, The, by Anne Johnson and Vic Goodman. New York: The Crossroad Publishing Company, 1995.

501 Ways to Boost Your Child's Self-Esteem by Robert D. Ramsey. Chicago: Contemporary Books, Inc., 1994.

Full Esteem Ahead by Diane Loomans with Julia Loomans. Tiburon, Calif.: H J Kramer Inc, 1994.

Help! The Kids Are at It Again: Using Kid's Quarrels to Teach "People" Skills by Elizabeth Crary. Seattle: Parenting Press, Inc., 1997.

How to Talk So Kids Will Listen & Listen So Kids Will Talk by Adele Faber and Elaine Mazlich. New York: Avon Books, 1980.

I'm on Your Side by Jane Nelsen, Ed.D. and Lynn Lott, M.A., M.F.C.C. Rocklin, Calif.: Prima Publishing, 1990.

Kid's Book of Questions, The, by Gregory Stock, Ph.D. New York: Workman Publishing, 1988.

Language of Letting Go, The, by Melody Beattie. New York: HarperCollins Publishers, 1990.

Maintaining Sanity in the Classroom: Classroom Management Techniques by Rudolf Dreikurs, M.D., Bernice Bronia Grunwald, and Floy C. Pepper. New York: HarperCollins Publishers, 1982.

Making Peace in Your Stepfamily by Harold H. Bloomfield, M.D. New York: Hyperion, 1993.

Our Journey Home: What Parents Are Doing to Preserve Family Values by Gary Bauer. Dallas: Word Publishing, 1992.

Parent's Little Book of Lists, The, by Jane Bluestein, Ph.D. Deerfield Beach, Florida: Health Communications, Inc., 1997.

Positive Parenting by Jane Nelsen, Lynn Lott and H. Stephen Glenn. Rocklin, Calif.: Prima Publishing, 1993.

Punished by Rewards by Alfie Kohn. Boston: Houghton Mifflin Company, 1993.

Raising Self-Reliant Children in a Self-Indulgent World by H. Stephen Glenn and Jane Nelsen, Ed.D. Rocklin, Calif.: Prima Publishing, 1989.

Raising Your Spirited Child by Mary Sheedy Kurcinka. New York: Harper Perennial, 1992.

Reviving Ophelia: Saving the Selves of Adolescent Girls by Mary Pipher, Ph.D. New York: Ballantine Books, 1995.

Temperament Tools: Working with Your Child's Inborn Traits by Helen Neville, R.N. and Diane Clark Johnson, C.F.L.E. Seattle: Parenting Press, Inc., 1998.

Wonderful Ways to Love a Child by Judy Ford. Berkeley: Conari Press, 1996.

Wonderful Ways to Love a Teen by Judy Ford. Berkeley: Conari Press, 1996

Your Child's Self-Esteem by Dorothy Corkille Briggs. New York: Doubleday, 1970.

Your One-Year-Old by Louise Bates Ames, Ph.D. and Carol Chase Haber, M.A. New York: Dell Publishing, 1989. (Series continues with books covering each age up to fourteen years.)

Index

About the Author

Kathryn J. Kvols is president of International Network for Children and Families, a company she started twenty years ago (under a different name at that time) to educate parents in the theories and techniques of peaceful parenting. Her life has been richly filled as a mental health counselor, a presenter of personal growth workshops, and a director of a summer camp for children that emphasized responsible behavior and self-esteem. Ms. Kvols serves on the board of the Montessori Foundation.

About 350 instructors teach the material found in *Redirecting Children's Behavior* all over the United States and in nine countries abroad.

Ms. Kvols and her husband have a blended family of five children ranging in age from 20's down to preschool age. Her experiences in a two-parent family, as a single mother, and as a stepmother now have given her insights into the challenges faced by many parents in today's changing society.

ↄ

Redirecting Children's Behavior Parenting Course

International Network for Children and Families provides resources for parenting courses and instructor training worldwide.

Evening Course

Small groups with hands-on learning; no lectures.

Classes meet one evening per week for five weeks.

Workbook and reference book included with course fee.

Call International Network for Children and Families for information on courses near you, or to find out how you can become a parent education instructor, at 800-257-9002.

You may also check Website http://www.redirectingbehavior.com/.

Books for Parents

Love & Limits: Guidance Tools for Creative Parenting by Elizabeth Crary introduces a simple problem-solving process known as STAR Parenting. Talks about kids' development and temperament traits, and offers practical guidance tools. Useful with kids birth to 8 years old. 48 pages, $6.95 paper, $16.95 library binding

Pick Up Your Socks . . . and Other Skills Growing Children Need! by Elizabeth Crary. Illustrated by Pati Casebolt. This book shows parents how to teach responsibility. A job chart listing average ages kids do household chores helps reduce unrealistic expectations. Useful with kids 3–12 years old. 112 pages, $14.95 paper, $19.95 library binding

Kids Can Cooperate: A Practical Guide to Teaching Problem Solving by Elizabeth Crary describes how to give children the skills to solve conflicts themselves. Includes a step-by-step process to help school-aged kids negotiate. Dialogues show problem solving in action. Useful with kids 3–12 years old. 104 pages, $12.95 paper, $19.95 library binding

Grounded for Life?! Stop Blowing Your Fuse and Start Communicating with Your Teenager by Louise Felton Tracy, M.A. A mother of six and a longtime middle school counselor, Tracy shows parents how to communicate effectively with their children. Useful with kids 10–18 years old. *Parents' Choice* award winner. 164 pages, $12.95 paper, $19.95 library binding

Ask for these books at your favorite bookstore, or call toll free 1-800-992-6657. VISA and MasterCard accepted with phone orders. Complete book catalog available on request.

Parenting Press, Inc.

Dept. 804, P.O. Box 75267, Seattle, WA 98125
In Canada, call Raincoast Books Distribution Co.,
1-800-663-5714

Prices subject to change without notice